Church and Family: Growing Together

# CHURCH AND FAMILY GROWING TOGETHER

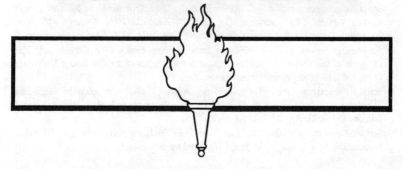

## John C. Howell

**BROADMAN PRESS**
Nashville, Tennessee

© Copyright 1984 • Broadman Press
All rights reserved
4256-62
ISBN: 0-8054-5662-7
Dewey Decimal Classification: 259
Subject Headings: CHURCH WORK WITH FAMILIES / / FAMILY
Library of Congress Catalog Card Number: 84-5007
Printed in the United States of America

**Library of Congress Cataloging in Publication Data**

Howell, John C.
  Church and family.

  Bibliography: p.
  1. Church work with families.   2. Family—Religious
life.   I. Title.
BV4438.H68   1984          259          84-5007
ISBN 0-8054-5662-7 (pbk.)

*To our grandson,*
*John Christian Howell II,*
*who has helped me rediscover*
*the excitement and joy*
*of growing up in a world*
*to be experienced and conquered*

# Preface

My interest in family needs was first awakened under the teaching of Dr. T. B. Maston at Southwestern Baptist Theological Seminary while pursuing my first graduate degree. Moving into the doctoral program in Christian Ethics, that interest was stimulated even more by experiencing the warm fellowship of the Maston home and by the opportunity to serve as chaplain and counselor for the Volunteers of America Maternity Home in Fort Worth, Texas.

Since that early beginning over thirty years ago, I have watched and been involved in the growing acceptance of family ministry as an essential part of the church's ministry to society. My pilgrimage in family understanding has been enriched by friendship with David and Vera Mace, Howard Clinebell, R. Lofton Hudson, and others who have shaped the direction of family life education and ministry in this country. Opportunities to participate in significant family life programs have been provided by the Family Ministry Department of The Sunday School Board of the Southern Baptist Convention (SBC). The students in my family ministry classes as well as the faculty and administration of Midwestern Baptist Theological Seminary have encouraged my concern for enriching family life. To all of these I express appreciation.

The skillful secretarial ministry of Mrs. Elaine Goode and Mrs. Jan Lundy made it possible for this book to reach its publishers in creditable form. I am grateful to them.

At the heart of it all, however, I am thankful for my own family members who have ministered to me with their love and understanding as I have sought to minister to others. Theories have been tested and partnership has grown in the almost forty years that Doris and I have experienced our own marriage enrichment. Our sons Michael and Mark together with Debera, our daughter by marriage, have been a source of fulfillment to us. They have helped me stay realistically in touch with what family can be as I share my own perceptions of family life with others.

It is an honor to be invited to participate in this Christian Leadership series of Broadman Press with a book on family ministry. My intention is to help ministers and laypersons in churches which currently do not have planned family ministry programs to see the possibilities for beginning that ministry now. If the book also is helpful to churches presently expanding their work with families, I will feel that the project has been a fulfillment of a long-time dream for our churches.

# Contents

# 1
# Church and Family: Partners in Ministry

A young mother came to the pastor and visiting family life educator before the evening conference began to invite us to share refreshments with her family after church. The invitation was gladly accepted. After the conclusion of the service, however, the pastor and I were called away to an emergency situation without being able to tell the host family about the change in plans.

Dealing with the emergency took over an hour and then the pastor insisted that we go to the home where we had been invited for refreshments. In spite of my protest, we knocked on the door and were greeted by the puzzled wife who had expected us much earlier. She accepted the pastor's story of our change in plans and invited us in. Her husband, she said, had gone to bed but would get up and join us. This increased my anxiety about being there at all!

Shortly after our visit began, the minister's wife (who was home with a sick child) called to tell him of a transient at the parsonage asking for help. He insisted that I stay and left with a promise to return quickly. My discomfort was now at a very high level.

The visit turned into a beautiful experience as I listened to the testimony of how the young husband and wife became Christians and began serving God in their home and church.

At the time of their wedding, neither were Christians. After a few years, two children had been added to the home along with plenty of daily bickering and fussing. In the midst of their struggles, they decided that their home needed some religion to help them get along better. Instead of going to a church, they bought a Bible and began to read it

aloud to each other. They prayed and asked God for direction. Through
their study of the Bible and prayer, they accepted Christ right in their
own living room.

Then they began looking for a church in which they could develop
their newfound faith. The local Baptist church took them into its
fellowship, baptized them, and nurtured their faith through love. Now
they were active members of the church which had become a partner
with their home in the fulfillment of Christian life. It was truly a
partnership in mission for their family.

The church and the family are partners in more ways than you might
realize. For example, social attitudes toward church and family showed
similar fluctuations from affirmation to rejection to renewed appreciation during the last half of this century.

During the early 1900s, the church was generally accorded a place of
honor and purpose; but in the 1950s, even theologians were despairing
about the effectiveness and potential viability of local churches. Believing that the churches were culture-bound and unable to proclaim
courageously the gospel of social concern as well as personal redemption, sincere Christians were convinced that the church existed like froth
on the ocean of life and that the pulpit was what Gerald Kennedy called
the "pit of harmlessness." Consequently, many believers were ready to
consign the churches to the role of cultural clubs having no importance
for committed Christian ministry. Community and social agencies were
believed to be better places for meeting human needs.

Changes in these attitudes during the late sixties and seventies were
reflected in the various Gallup poll samples of public opinion about the
importance of the church in society. For many persons the church was
reinstated as essential to the proclamation and demonstration of the
whole gospel of personal redemption coupled with social concern.
Ministry to the human needs of persons assumed a new importance in
the church at the same time that the emergence of new forms of
evangelism developed to reach nonbelievers at all levels of cultural
experience.

Thus attitudes toward the church changed from early affirmation to a sense of despair for its survival followed by a renewed appreciation for its potential witness to our contemporary world. The family has traveled a similar pathway in the American cultural scene.

Immediately following World War II, young people responded to the popular belief that marriage was the normative pattern of life by marrying at an early age and in abundant numbers. The average age for marriage in 1950 was 22.8 for boys and 20.3 for girls. More girls married at 18 than any other age. According to a Gallup poll in 1968, the majority of respondents believed that the ideal family should include the mother and father plus four children.

In spite of the high divorce rate of 4.3 divorces per 1,000 adult population in 1946, the year following the end of WW II, marriage was generally accepted as a permanent relationship. From 1946 to 1950 the divorce rate dropped to 2.3 per 1,000 adult population and remained fairly close to that figure for about 17 years. Marriage and family seemed secure and acceptable.

During the late sixties and early seventies, however, marriage and family came under severe attacks from the children born during the baby boom following WW II. Criticism of family values, of sexual mores, and of parenting styles were acted out in the rejection of the nuclear family as a desirable setting for personal wholeness. Communes, living together without marriage, and more extensive and younger involvement in sexual experience were all praised as preferable to the traditional ideal of premarital chastity and monogamous marriage. For those who were married, the ideal number of desired children dropped from four in 1968 to two in 1973. Divorce resumed its upward surge in 1967 which has resulted in over one million divorces per year being granted since 1977. Sociologists and family analysts both in and out of the churches joined in a litany of despair for the survival of the traditional family.

Granted that contemporary families in the United States (and other parts of the world) do confront a vast array of social and personal threats to fulfilling survival, it does appear that marriage and family are valued much higher now than was true a decade ago. Witness the fact that approximately 80 percent of persons who divorce remarry within five years. The traditional marriage ceremony performed in the church has regained its popularity. The *rate* of divorce has declined even though the number remains high. Approximately two-thirds of American couples are living in their first and only marriage relationship.

Thus attitudes toward the family, as well as the church, have moved along a spectrum of affirmation, rejection, and renewed appreciation during the last half of this century. Church and family are certainly partners in confronting such diverse attitude changes in our time. But what are some of the fundamental factors involved in declaring that church and family are partners *in mission*? Let me suggest some significant illustrations of this partnership.

## The Church and Family Share a Common Origin

Christians interpret the biblical revelation of God's purpose for human life from many different perspectives. Generally, however, the Bible is affirmed as the written record of God's revelation of himself, of the relationship possible between God and persons, and of the relationship intended between persons in God's plan for human life. Believing that the Bible provides insight into all phases of human experience, we can see, first, that the family has its beginning in accord with God's purpose for man and woman.

### The Family: The Work of God in Creation

In the beautiful symbolism of Genesis 2:18-24, the marital relationship is based upon God's awareness of the need for companionship between man and woman. The text is sometimes used to defend a superior-inferior interpretation of the male-female relationship, but this is not actually inferred by the passage. Woman was created as a companion after no other creature offered to man a fitting fulfillment of his need for social interaction. She was made as one who corresponded to him or one who was like him, not as one designed only to be his need-meeter or subordinate to him. As man and woman together they were called Man (Gen. 5:2) and were to meet each other's needs. They were to become one flesh in a shared experience of sexual and emotional self-giving to each other. This was pictured as God's original intention for the marital union.

Jesus reaffirmed this purpose of God in his controversy with the Pharisees about divorce which is recorded in Matthew 19:3-9 and Mark 10:2-12. After reminding the Pharisees of God's establishment of marriage as a one-flesh union, Jesus declared, "What therefore God has joined together, let no man put asunder" (Matt. 19:6). I understand this to mean that God purposed marriage as a human relationship that would last, not that we are to try to determine which particular marriages are God-ordained. Thus the family is God's first creative work for human fulfillment and must have significant importance in our ministry to social needs.

### The Church: The Work of God in Re-Creation

Just as God brought the family into being in the beginning of human life, so he established the church for nurturing those who experience re-creation through faith in Jesus Christ. Jesus gave us a clear statement of this new life experience when he declared to Peter, "On this rock I will build my church, and the powers of death shall not prevail against it" (Matt. 16:18). The church, like the family, is a social institution that has evolved over long years of Christian history and, as such, can be studied by historians and sociologists. Its membership and customs reflect cultural conditioning in the various sections of the country and the world. It is a part of our society.

But the church is also more than that. As a community of faith, it was established by God to fulfill his purposes in the world, and it is still sustained by him. It is often limited by human frailty and sin, but it is essential to the life of faith and to the fulfilling of God's commission to serve as a reconciling force in human relationships—the relationship between God and persons as well as the relationships between persons.

Paul highlighted this reconciling ministry of the church in his powerful word to the Corinthians: "All this is from God, who through Christ reconciled us to himself and gave us the ministry of reconciliation; that is, in Christ God was reconciling the world unto himself, not counting their trespasses against them, and entrusting to us the message of reconciliation" (2 Cor. 5:18-19). On the basis of one's reconciliation with God, there is also to be a spirit of reconciliation in the interpersonal relations with others in the church and, by implication, in the family. To the Ephesians Paul wrote, "Let all bitterness and wrath and anger and clamor and slander be put away from you, with all malice, and be kind to one another, tenderhearted, forgiving one another, as God in Christ forgave you" (4:31-32).

The family and the church have their common origin, therefore, in the creative purpose of the Father. Since this is true, they bear equally the need for support in the Christian community and should be looked upon as mutual allies in God's redemptive concern for human life in all of its fullness. As human institutions, however, church and family also face similar concerns in society as they seek to fulfill their reconciling function.

## The Church and Christian
## Family Face Similar Social Concerns

An extended discussion of these social concerns would require a book in itself, but let me suggestively examine some conflicting social philosophies which confront church and family with significant challenges.

Our philosophies about life reflect the thought patterns and values which guide our choices and behavior. In the nation today, there are a number of social philosophies conflicting with each other that have sizable groups of supporters.

### Personal Freedom Versus Authoritarianism

The nation was founded on the premise of responsible personal freedom for the majority of the people in the belief that informed persons would act in ways that would further the national life. Baptist churches have defended that principle for their own church life, as well as for the nation. In recent years, however, irresponsible use of personal freedom by some has created a social trend toward authoritarianism in government, in society, and in church relationships. Prominent ministers argue for an authoritarian ministry in which the pastor speaks the final word of God for the congregation. Religious and political leaders desire power to restrict personal freedoms in such sensitive areas as marital sexuality, abortion, and sexual preference. Seminar leaders and religious authors demand a male-dominant family structure as the only authentically Christian one. Church and family alike are caught up in the struggle to achieve a responsible balance between personal freedom and authoritarianism.

## Individualism Versus Mutuality

Pioneer America celebrated the strong individual who could achieve success in conquering the new world and the new west on his own terms. The perspective of individualism born in that early struggle has continued to dominate the American scene. While honoring the ability to achieve, it has also been a roadblock to mutual interdependence since this might be looked upon as a weakness. Philip E. Slater, in *The Pursuit of Loneliness,* establishes a good case for viewing extreme individualism as one of the reasons we remain thwarted in our desire to create community at the same time that we refuse to give up our privacy as persons. It is a sad commentary on our life-style that fear of crime among some apartment dwellers has created more mutual interdependence than has been achieved by churches or governments.

Individualism in the churches may also keep members from becoming a functioning "body of Christ" in the way the New Testament described it. Individualism in the family, especially as men subscribe to the masculinity of the frontier philosophy, may keep family members from achieving a close and fulfilling intimacy in the family.

## Sexual Equality Versus Sexual Subordination

The defeat of the Equal Rights Amendment in the legislature of America in 1982 does not mean the end of struggles over equality between the sexes. Political battles over equal pay for equal work, equal opportunity for jobs, and a host of other issues will remain with us for a long time. Our concern in this section, however, is the impact of this struggle on church and family.

Women ministers, ordination of women as deacons, and the place of women in the teaching functions of the churches highlight the struggle going on in local churches and denominations. Withdrawal of fellowship and cries of biblical heresy greet churches that dare to move in the direction of sexual equality in church ministries.

As mentioned earlier, family life education is caught up in the struggle over role definition in the home based upon cultural characteristics of the family in the biblical world which place the woman in the home rather than in the business world. In spite of the argument that male dominance in the family does not imply female subordination, adherents of companionship-style marriages believe that it does. Thus church and family alike are involved in the debate over sexual equality.

## Materialistic Values Versus Spiritual Values

It is impossible to escape pressures toward measuring successful living against the standard of materialism if one listens to television, reads newspaper ads, or attends a business-sponsored seminar on the achieving life. This seems also to be true in some presentations of "how to be successful in church growth" techniques! Here again the church and family face similar concerns.

In recent years, Southern Baptist church life has witnessed an upswing in the number of ministers released or fired by their churches. One of the factors appears to be the failure of the minister to produce expected growth in members and finances during his tenure in office. Rather than examine the church's standard of measureable values, the church releases the minister and searches for one who can be more "successful." In saying this, I recognize that some situations are clear evidences of ministerial lack of ability or integrity, but a number are not. Materialistic values have overcome spiritual values in many situations.

Families have not escaped this pressure to evaluate the good life in terms of material gains with a possible failure to find emotional and spiritual happiness in the process. It is not unusual for a newly married couple to spend so much time, as well as physical and emotional energy, earning sufficient money to buy the things they feel they need that either they lose each other or never establish a healthy intimacy in their marriage. The statistic that first marriages ending in divorce in the United States do so at about 6.8 years after marriage may speak to this point.

## The Church and Christian
## Family Share Common Objectives

Against this backdrop of challenging social concerns, the church and the Christian family also share some common objectives in developing persons for creative life together. Let us examine four objectives which can be implemented most successfully in the family-church partnership

### Meaningful Worship

A first shared objective is to lead their members into meaningful experiences with God. This objective focuses on the fact that worship is a necessity for Christian growth and that worship is a family possibility, as well as a church responsibility. I am using the term *worship* to include all ways in which individuals in the church and family experience the presence of God in their lives and respond to that presence in devotion and service. The psalmist set an appropriate tone for such worship experiences when he invited, "O come, let us worship and bow down,/ let us kneel before the Lord, our Maker!/ For he is our God,/ and we are the people of his pasture,/ and the sheep of his hand" (95:6). Jesus emphasized the central commitment of worship in his response to the Tempter, "Begone, Satan! for it is written,/ 'You shall worship the Lord your God/ and him only shall you serve'" (Matt. 4:10).

Within the varied activities of a typical church program, the presence of God may be experienced in the formal worship services on Sunday or in the informality of a campfire service at a retreat setting. God meets us in many and varied ways, sometimes in a manner that is different from our expectations. Moses met God when he turned in curiosity to examine a burning bush. Elijah heard God in the quietness of a still small voice after expecting to find him in the powerfulness of earthquake and fire. Peter responded to the presence of God in the midst of his humiliation and dejection for having denied his Savior.

The family may also experience God's presence in many ways. Children, as well as parents, often hear God's voice in the regularly scheduled times of family worship when the Bible is read and explained to the gathered family. But God is also present in the fun times of the family at play and in the spontaneous, awe-inspiring moments that happen without planning or anticipation. These may be moments of joy in a birthday, of response to the beauty of a shared sunrise, or even to a significant event of sorrow. Christian worship celebrates what God has given us in Christ—hope, new life, and fellowship.

Church and family, therefore, respond to the desire for human life to be enriched and inspired by experiencing the presence of God as they individually plan ways to develop more meaningful worship times. When church members and family members alike can declare with Job, "I had heard of thee by the hearing of the ear, but now my eye sees thee" (42:5), this objective is being fulfilled in life.

## Purposeful Relationships

Providing a setting where people may learn how to live creatively and purposefully with each other is a second shared objective. The home is always a first school of relationships. Husband and wife must learn how to adapt their differences and reinforce their similarities in order to create a complementary relationship. Stress may occur because of personality differences, inter-family conflicts, time prioritizing and interest-managing decisions, and spiritual growth goals. Parents and children can conflict over disciplinary styles, home responsibilities, and use of the family car. Couple conflicts and intergenerational differences are normal in our society, but they do test the ability of the family to learn how to resolve conflicts, as well as to enhance togetherness.

Churches are also schools of relationship in which people are encouraged to live creatively and purposefully with each other. Paul's word to the Colossian Christians points to the type of life which we would all like to see in the church: "Put on then, as God's chosen ones, holy and beloved, compassion, kindness, lowliness, meekness, and patience, forbearing one another and, if one has a complaint against another, forgiving each other; as the Lord has forgiven you, so you also must forgive. And above all these put on love, which binds everything together in perfect harmony" (3:12-14).

As we read the New Testament, however, we know that the church also had difficulties in establishing the harmony that Paul encouraged. In the Corinthian church there was dissension, quarreling, and drunkenness. Euodia and Synteche were at odds with each other in the Philippian church, and the Galatian Christians were caught up in a doctrinal controversy. Even in the company of devoted believers there was conflict and struggle.

Are we to conclude, therefore, that home and church are failures in helping people to learn to live with each other? Not at all! Conflict demonstrates our humanity, but God's grace enables us to become loving fellowships within which we can learn to live with other people as growing persons. We can practice our faith in the family, as well as in the church, as we express love, practice forgiveness, accept responsibility, and affirm one another. The word of Paul to the Roman church helps us here: "Let love be genuine; hate what is evil, hold fast to what is good; love one another with brotherly affection; outdo one another in showing honor" (12:9-10).

In his call for authentic Christian love, Paul used the word *agape,* the love that demonstrates itself in a concern for the other person which becomes greater than the concern for self. In his encouragement of mutual affection, he used a combination word which includes friendship love (*philia*) and family love (*storge*). When these qualities of love dominate life in the family and the church, the objective of learning to live together can be accomplished.

## Family-Centered Evangelism

The challenge of extending the witness of God's love to others in need of Christ is a third shared objective of church and home. Evangelism is the sharing of the good news of the gospel from one person to another with the purpose of encouraging a decision for Christ as Savior and Lord in the life of the unbelieving person. Many churches are regularly engaged in evangelistic outreach through visitation programs, lay witness activities, revival services, regular worship times, and other social service programs designed to minister to persons in times of need. Most churches would probably agree that this is an important objective for being the church today.

Perhaps you have not considered evangelism also as an objective for the family, but it can legitimately be affirmed as an opportunity for extending the gospel to other families. In a Baptist Sunday School Board publication entitled *Your Family: A Witness for Christ,* the writers point out that "the concept of one family reaching another is not new; you may find families in your church who have this vision already. The vision may be buried, however, because so few families know how to implement it."[1] In discussing families sharing their faith with other families, the authors invite family members to evaluate what special qualities of family faith and experience each family might have that would be valuable to share with others. Then the families are encouraged to select families with whom they might share their faith and proceed to develop ways of relating to those families.

An Iowa family became a witnessing group several years ago after becoming Christians during a revival in a local church. The husband and wife had been included in a group of couples who met regularly on Saturday nights in the homes of group members for parties involving drinking and some sexual explorations. After their conversion the couple could no longer be a part of this group, but they did decide to use their home as a setting for outreach to others. As new families moved into their neighborhood, they would welcome them with coffee and cake, invite the newcomers to their home for a meal, and offer any help they could to the family. They quietly inquired about the religious situation of the new family and told them about the churches of their denominational affiliation in the area. If the newcomers were not Christians, they offered their own church as a place of welcome and volunteered to pick them up for the services. Based on their friendly and warm-hearted concern, a door was opened to share their faith in Christ as well. During one six-month period, five families were received into the fellowship of their church through conversion or transfer of church membership. Families can let their homes fulfill the objectives of personal witness to the gospel of Jesus Christ in a shared partnership with their church.[2]

## Ministry to Others

The final shared objective which we will consider is to involve their members in ministry to the needs of other persons. Ministry has been defined as a "helping response to humanity's hurt and search for wholeness."[3] In this context, we are concerned with the helping offer extended to persons either in or outside of the church who have social, emotional, and/or physical needs to which church members or families could respond appropriately.

The mandate for such concern was clearly set forth by Jesus in his affirmation of the calling given to him by the Father. In his synagogue at Nazareth, Jesus read from Isaiah, "The Spirit of the Lord is upon me,/ because he has anointed me to preach good news to the poor./ He has sent me to proclaim release to the captives/ and recovering of sight to the blind,/ to set at liberty those who are oppressed,/ to proclaim the acceptable year of the Lord." He then declared, "Today this scripture has been fulfilled in your hearing" (Luke 4:18-19,21). Luke later records Peter's testimony to Jesus as one who "went about doing good and healing all who were oppressed" (Acts 10:38).

The early church demonstrated its active concern for the physical needs of its members in Jerusalem (Acts 4:32-37), as well as in the love offering received by Paul to aid the Jerusalem church in a time of famine (2 Cor. 8—9). Church members were rebuked by John (1 John 3:16-18) and James (Jas. 2:15-17) for failure to aid the needy. Jesus described God's judgment on those who neglected the hurts of their neighbors (Matt. 25:31-46). The ministry of the church to needy persons has a compelling and clear mandate in the New Testament and is a worthy objective in ministry.

Families also can be involved in this helping ministry to human need. Let me cite one illustration of this ministry from *How to Minister to Families in Your Church.*

> Sara, a single parent, lost her job. She found herself faced with the problem of finding a cheaper apartment, feeding her two children and herself, securing school clothes for her older child—and finding a new job.
>
> The Wilson family—who had not known her previously—were asked by the church to come to her rescue. Ralph Wilson helped her in her contacts with public-housing authorities. Mrs. Wilson took Sara to the church for groceries from the church ministry pantry. Sara's ten-year-old was outfitted for school with clothes too small for the fast-growing Sam Wilson, and Mrs. Wilson found a neighbor who shared with Sara's preschooler clothes outgrown by her child.
>
> When Sara went for a job interview, the Wilsons' teenage daughter sat with her children to save babysitting fees. The entire Wilson family became involved at the time of Sara's need. They cared.[4]

Such family concern for others may be expressed through ministry in times of death, to older persons who need companionship in programs such as Adopt a Grandparent, to shut-ins who need phone calls and some indication that they still have worth as persons, and to persons in need of physical care through providing food, house repair, or clothing. Churches can help equip families for ministry and alert them to families in need. Through this ministry the family and the church truly become partners in mission.[5]

This partnership based upon common origins, shared concerns, and common objectives can become a reality as ministers and churches take seriously the challenge of family ministry programs in the church.

# 2
# The Church's Mission to Families

The planning committee for a two-state family life conference to be conducted on the campus of Midwestern Baptist Theological Seminary several years ago was discussing alternative themes for the conference. Several of the committee members wanted the theme to emphasize ways in which families and family members could more effectively support the organizational life of the church. After long deliberation, however, the committee chose a theme which focused the conference agenda on ways the churches could strengthen families. They concluded that the family was primary in its needs and in its importance to human life.

It seems to me that this must be the approach to take in our ministry, even though I have already described how the church and family can be partners in mission to each other. The family is God's first institution for human development, and it needs all the support which churches can give to it. This is especially true today when family experiences are so varied and family needs are so great. This chapter will examine some of the targets for family ministry as the church fulfills its mission to families.

## The Church's Mission to the Family Unit

The dominant individualism in American culture mentioned in chapter 1 has influenced the understanding which many Christians have had concerning the Christian experience and the place of families in the church. Conversion has been interpreted in very individualistic terms. Salvation is an individual's response to God's invitation to faith that has little to do with the human relationships in which the convert lives.

Personal security is the essential consequence of conversion, and this can be achieved with little consideration being given to family, job, or society. From this perspective, a family is primarily viewed as a collection of individuals who need to be converted and integrated into church life as independent persons.

When I first became a pastor in 1950, my denomination placed a very strong emphasis on evangelism. The community religious census was promoted as the means for discovering prospects for church membership, and our church entered into this program enthusiastically. However, we were hardly conscious at that time of a terrible flaw in our census procedure. As the census takers secured information about a family's religious affiliations, the name of each family member was put on a separate card.

These cards were turned in to the church office. Assignments were then made to the various Sunday School departments to visit the family member whose age made him or her a prospect for that department. No attempt was made to provide information about the spiritual condition of other family members since the departmental concern was dealing with the individual prospect. No effort was made to understand the family as a unit—it was only a collection of individuals.

Fortunately this procedure changed after a few years, and all census information for each family was placed on a family record card. In many cases, however, church leaders still fail to understand the family as a unit with needs and problems of its own. Instead, they view the family as the spawning place for individuals who can be enrolled in choirs, classes, committees, and other organizational structures of church life. Calendar planning, organizational meetings, and multi-night activities give little or no consideration to the family's need for time together to play, work, or rediscover the meaning of a home together! Even so-called "family nights" at church often assign children to their rooms, adolescents to theirs, and parents or other adults to their own session as couples are separated as male and female.

Social psychologists have insisted that the unit is always greater than the sum of its individual parts. A family has an identity and life of its own which churches must recognize when planning programs and activities for the membership. Unnecessarily pulling families apart is not a healthy way to encourage family growth and stability when it is done on a regular basis in calendar planning for the year.

In a church where I was interim pastor, the most common criticism of the former pastor was his insensitivity to family relationships when he called meetings. Being in a downtown location, many of the leaders drove some distance to come to church. It was not unusual for the pastor to call a meeting of deacons or other leadership people late on Sunday afternoon. Following the meeting, several had to drive back home to pick up their families and return to church. These leaders felt that the called meetings too often dealt with matters that could have been handled by phone or by a smaller committee, but their main criticism was timing. Instead of planning the meetings when the families would be present anyway, leaders were pulled away from their families on the one day they could be together at home. Inadequate advance planning and lack of appreciation for family needs were at the heart of the issue.

Another illustration of failure to value the family unit involves a church staff which makes little or no effort to coordinate calendaring in such a way that family time is protected. Each staff member is free to "do his own thing" and resents any suggestion that his thing may be creating serious conflicts for families who are conscientious in supporting the full church program. One church evaluated its programming and decided to discontinue Sunday night services at the church in an effort to encourage families to use that evening for family activities. Barely six weeks after this decision was advertised widely to the membership, the youth choir director decided that Sunday evening would make an ideal time for youth choir rehearsals. When this was announced, families were justifiably confused about coordination in church planning!

Understanding that the family has needs as a unit encourages the church to plan various activities which can help solidify family togetherness. For example, family enrichment experiences, such as a camping retreat, family-centered picnic, or family retreat using a program of separate sessions by age combined with joint sessions for whole families, can be planned. It has been said with some degree of truth that the family which prays together will stay together. It is even more true that families who pray *and play* together have a greater sense of fulfillment and intimacy in their relationships.

New techniques in marital and family therapy are also becoming aware that family units develop systems of interaction which affect the emotional and spiritual health of the family members. Ministers and other counselors recognize that seeing each member of the family separately gives a slanted perspective on the operating style of the family when it is together. Consequently some counselors bring the whole family into the counseling sessions at least part of the time in order to discover how the various family members interact with each other. These counselors become aware very quickly that the whole is greater than the sum of its individual parts!

Whether the unit under consideration is a family of once-married parents and their children, single parents, blended families, or adult couples whose children have left the nest, churches need to give attention to ways of ministry that can strengthen the unit. This is one aspect of the church's mission to the family.

## The Church's Mission
## to Individuals Living in Families

Having emphasized strongly the necessity of giving attention to the needs of the family unit, it is also necessary to recognize that individuals within the family have significant needs of their own. The needs of couples without children are different from the needs of parents with young children. Older children face different life situations than teenagers, and senior adults ask different questions than median adults. Two-parent families experience different parenting problems than single parents.

In order to accomplish its mission to persons living in such diverse types of marriage and family situations, careful analysis of the family styles present in the church membership must be made. When one

Kansas City church did an age-related study of its membership, over 300 members in the 65-plus age range were identified. Immediate steps were taken to provide a ministry to individuals and couples in that age spectrum. Another Missouri church found that its membership and potential membership in the community included a significant number of single parents who needed day-care services for their children. They responded by employing a preschool children's worker and by establishing a day-care service.

In our society, it appears that women are provided more opportunities for group discussions about marriage and family issues than are offered to men as husbands and fathers. In over two-hundred church-sponsored family enrichment programs that I have conducted, we have included a separate session for men. A number of these men have remarked that it was the first time they had ever had a chance to discuss candidly and openly some of their joys and fears in being husbands and fathers. Men need such a time for processing feelings apart from their mates and families.

Women are struggling with the vast changes that have occurred in male-female roles during recent years. Churches can provide a forum for discussion and study that can help wives and mothers become more secure in the changing roles either thrust upon them or chosen by them. The rapid increase in the number of dual-income or dual-career families is creating a strange kind of double-bind situation for many Christian women. The wife with small children who works away from the home may feel very guilty about her job because she must have others care for her children while she works. She feels she should be staying home even if she is working because of economic necessity. At times, the emphasis of the church on woman's homemaker role has accentuated her guilt unnecessarily.

On the other hand, the wife who is a homemaker may feel guilty because she is not producing an income by outside employment. She has been exposed to so much emphasis on the importance of having a career for self-fulfillment or economic security that she feels guilty for staying home with the children.

Through open and honest discussion with other women under sympathetic leadership, wives in each category may be helped to resolve their guilt and feel more confident in their decision concerning working out of the home or staying at home. Christian freedom to choose wisely can be encouraged.

Primarily because of the high divorce rate, there are currently about nine million single parent families in the United States with most of them having a mother as head of the household. In such situations, the custodial parent as well as the non-custodial parent and the children each have distinctive needs to which churches can respond.

Research studies have shown that children involved in divorced families seldom have an opportunity to discuss their feelings of anger and of felt responsibility for the divorce of their parents. In addition these children and young people may need help in finding ways to relieve the stress of living in a one-parent home with a working parent, as well as adjusting to visits with the non-custodial parent. Churches often have organizational resources to provide such opportunities if the leadership is aware of the need.

Blended families, those families created by persons who remarry after death or divorce of a mate, may include his, hers, and their children resulting in potentially stressful relationships between the parents, between the children from different families, and between the parents and children. Once again the opportunity to air these conflicts in an accepting and reconciling atmosphere can be offered by churches who understand the problems involved.

Changing sexual mores present many churches with the new reality of responding to persons living together without being married but still coming to the services and programs of the church. During the 1983 meeting of the Southern Baptist Association of Family Ministers, one Texas member described the increasing frequency of dealing with situations where a divorced mother and her potential future husband lived together in her house from four to six months before marrying. In some of these homes, the whole family, including the live-in male, would have regular devotionals at bed-time. They were religiously active but living together without marriage. Such situations will probably become more common in the future, thus confronting churches with the challenge of ministering to such persons without approving of their live-in life-style.

Probably enough has been said to illustrate the fact that individuals living in family relationships also have significant needs which can become a focus for planning family ministry. The third category of persons who should be included are those who live alone.

## The Church's Mission to Persons Living Alone

Census reports indicate the increasing number of persons who constitute a one-person household in the United States. Such situations are created by delayed marriage among young adults, by the deliberate choice to remain unmarried, by divorce or death of a mate, and by the lack of opportunity for marriage when there is a desire to marry.

Each of these persons is related in some way to a primary family but at the present time is not living in a family setting. For the purpose of the family ministry program of a local church, however, they can be considered as individual family units rather than merely as households.

Age and the reason for living alone are significant factors in this category in assessing needs to which the church might respond in its family ministry program. Young adults pursuing career goals through extended education or initiating vocational involvements in business or industry have very different life experiences from senior adults who live alone because a mate has died after years of marriage. Divorced persons living alone are coping with different problems from never-marrieds who have chosen to be single as they come to grips with their own personal growth.

In spite of these differences, however, there are some issues which seem common to many persons living alone. One issue is the development of a healthy self-concept as a single adult. A single student expressed an attitude which I have found fairly common when he said, "One of my major problem areas is the poor self-image that I have of myself. I am my greatest critic and consequently harbor guilt and guilt feelings. This causes problems at times in relating to those who want to get close to me for I feel I would not be good for them." Self-identity was also fundamental in the reflections of a divorced woman who commented, "In the case of my previous marriage, if my husband and I had been adult persons with a good sense of identity, the marriage may have had better days. Both of us were not responsible persons."

A negative sense of self-worth often accompanies the feelings of failure involved in a divorce, especially for Christians. Singles who want to marry but have not had opportunity can feel rejected and unworthy. Family ministry programming can include specific opportunities for singles to understand and accept the new selfhood available in Jesus Christ through repentance and grace.

A second issue is the challenge of accepting and being comfortable with one's sexuality as a single. For those who have been married but now live alone, there is an abrupt cessation of regular sexual experiences, especially if the mate died suddenly. Even in marriages terminated by dissolution or divorce, there probably were fairly regular sexual relations until the actual time of separation. The divorced or widowed do not automatically become nonsexual in their feelings and desires because they live alone. Instead they must now face the difficult decisions, for some at least, with regard to handling these feelings in an appropriate Christian manner.

I remember vividly the first time this question was presented to me as a pastor. The husband of one of our active church members confronted her with his determination to divorce her. They had no children but had enjoyed an active and fulfilling sex life in the marriage. This part of their life together was very important to her. We sat one evening after church discussing her adjustment to the divorce situation. Suddenly she blurted out the question that startled me and challenged my thinking about separation, "What am I going to do about my sexual needs!" Never having faced that question before in talking with persons formerly married, I was unable to help her much at that time with an appropriate answer. Over the years of my pastoral and teaching ministry, I have concluded that we in the church are still unable or unwilling to grapple sensitively and redemptively with that question for the formerly married.

The younger never-marrieds have grown up in a culture where nonmarital sexual relationships are increasingly acceptable and experienced among a sizable proportion of the American population. They, therefore, have to determine the values and standards which will guide their own sexual behavior in their dating relationships. The church can provide discussion sessions which can help them establish these standards on a wholesome Christian foundation. Older never-marrieds may also need this kind of opportunity, but they have usually come to some acceptable adaptation of their behavior to their values by this time.

For all persons living alone there is also a third issue—loneliness. Contrast can be made between aloneness as a voluntary choice to withdraw from interpersonal contacts for a time in order to fulfill certain needs or desires and loneliness as an involuntary separation from persons that may not be our choice. Loneliness may be the result of fear as we feel some kind of vulnerability in being close to people. It may be the fear of being hurt emotionally or physically or the fear of being rejected by others. It may come as a consequence of loss, such as the death of a mate, close family member, or even a close friend. The loss of pets or possessions may also create intense feelings of loneliness for persons who live alone.

Bill Moulder, a single on the faculty of Trinity Evangelical Divinity School, comments graphically on his own experience of loneliness that speaks for many other singles. "What does it feel like to be lonely?" asks Moulder. "I think the word that best describes the feeling for me is *empty*. It feels as if there were a big hole right in the middle of my chest. . . . Loneliness hits me on Friday about five o'clock when I'm worn out from the week's work and want someone to relax with me, but I have to go home to an empty apartment."[1] The family ministry program of the church needs to recognize and help alleviate where possible the problem of loneliness.

Now that attention has been given to the family unit, to persons living in families, and to persons living alone as objects of family ministry, I want to suggest that the ministry can be shaped by responding to felt needs created by the developmental stages of personal growth and family life.

## The Church's Mission
## Through Developmental Stages

Two developmental themes are relevant to this section. One is the human developmental cycle from birth to old age, and the other is the family life cycle from singleness to marriage to singleness again. Each of these models of human interaction is important to the church's task in family ministry as it seeks to develop programs of education, enrichment, and ministry. Space limitations make it possible to give only a brief introduction to these approaches.

Psychologist Erik Erikson's portrayal of human life as movement through eight successive stages of psychosocial growth is a popular characterization of a developmental approach to human experience. He provides more specific guidance for understanding the crises and tasks of childhood through adolescence than he does for the adult years, but he does at least label the adult tasks. Greater attention has been given to adult developmental psychology in recent years by other authors. Samuel Levinson's *The Seasons of a Man's Life* and Gail Sheehy's *Passages* have popularized the age-related and task-related issues that affect adult behavior.

Christian ministers and counselors need not accept without question conclusions offered by these and other authors, but they can benefit from research concerning developmental stages as they plan educational and counseling methodologies to meet human need. Transition points from the thirties to the forties or from the forties to the fifties do have intense psychological meaning for many persons with regard to their selfhood, vocations, and family relationships. Awareness of potential stress times can alert the church to types of needs that family ministry programs may help alleviate

The family life cycle is the second model of human development which can be utilized profitably in planning family ministry. Even though the normative structure of the cycle may be interrupted by events in one's own family cycle, it does help to identify stages of family development to which specific ministry might be directed. A basic outline of the cycle is:

1. The single life—youth to adult
2. From engagement to marriage
3. From marriage to the first pregnancy
4. The child-bearing years—preschool children
5. The child-development years—early and middle school-age children
6. Adolescent children in the home
7. Launching pad years—children leaving home
8. The empty nest—children out of the home
9. Retirement for husband and wife
10. Death of a mate

Evelyn Duvall was an early explorer of this developmental approach to family studies. She declared, "The developmental task concept satisfied my search for a frame of reference that dealt dynamically with the challenge of human development, keeping responsibility in the hands of the developing persons, and still allowing room for the helping and assisting roles that family members, school personnel and community workers might play."[2]

The family life cycle utilizes the combination of personal development plus family life experiences as a framework for aiding growth. Since the New Testament is growth-oriented in its description of life under the lordship of Christ, adult psychological development and family cycle development can be related well to biblical patterns for life.

# 3
# Developing a Perspective on Family Ministry

Since family ministry is but one aspect of the total ministry of the church in its community, it is important to develop a perspective on this ministry in relationship to the church's larger task. If we think of the total ministry responsibility of the church as a picture of persons at work for Christ, family ministry must be blended into that picture in a manner appropriate to its own needs and contributions: It is not the whole picture, but it cannot be left out if our picture of ministry is to be complete.

When this is recognized, a pastor's comment on beginning such ministries will be answered. "Sure, I know that our church families are having problems, but we just don't have time to add any more programs to our crowded schedule!" This attitude is common but inaccurate. Adding another program is not the way to accomplish ministry to family needs. Instead, developing an appropriate perspective on family ministry involves a new way of looking at the ongoing program of the church. This perspective utilizes the regularly scheduled activities, as well as some specific activities focused on family needs.

For example, in scheduling its annual program of stewardship development and budget support, a church can include at least one session designed to help families deal more effectively with their own financial management in the home. The session could focus on the importance of and methods of will-making or on ways to develop family budgets. This approach enables a church to respond to family needs at the same time that it is meeting its own stewardship responsibilities in budget planning and pledging. Such planning requires a perspective on

family ministry which sees opportunities for family life education
throughout the annual calendar of activities.

At other times a church may include a specific family-oriented activity
in its calendar because of the felt need for such ministry. Evangelical
churches often include weeks of revival or evangelistic outreach in their
annual program of activities. In recent years some of these churches are
scheduling family enrichment conferences to take the place of one of the
revival periods. As one pastor explained, "We have come to see that our
own church people, as well as those outside of the church, need the
church's help in strengthening their homes. It is important that we meet
these needs, as well as reach out to evangelize our community. Our
people are used to coming to the church for meetings, so we decided to
focus on family needs for one week each year rather than use it for
revival in the traditional sense." The church's response to this different
approach was enthusiastic and affirming.

### Strategic Role of the Minister(s)

Obviously such planning as just described will occur only if the
pastor and staff have a positive perspective on family ministry as an
essential part of the church's program. Let us examine the strategic place
of the minister in developing family ministry emphases.

### Motivating and Equipping

At times the church's desire for guidance in family matters will surface
in a Sunday School class of young couples or among parents concerned
about their children. At other times it may come up for discussion in a
meeting of the planning council or official board. No matter how it
arises, the expressed need will seldom lead to action without the support
and encouragement of the vocational ministry staff and especially of the
pastor. In most of our churches, this means that the pastor must be a
motivator, encourager, and equipper who believes unreservedly that the
church does have a mission to families.

J. C. Wynn suggested some years ago that organizing one's pastoral
ministry around the family could provide "a lift instead of a load"! He

described much of the minister's work as "administrativia" which can become so fatiguing but offered family-life ministry as a renewing and rewarding opportunity in ministry. Such ministry includes two functional steps: (1) organizing one's daily work around the central theme of family ministry and (2) equipping parents and church leaders for their own involvement in the task.[1]

Many recent studies of family ministry have emphasized the inability of the vocational staff to accomplish all that is essential in a well-rounded ministry to family-related needs. Equipping God's people for their own work in ministry to persons is the only way many churches will be able effectively to use their human resources for education and ministry to families. In addition to being biblically sound (Eph. 4:11-12), equipping persons for ministry to persons is the most effective way for the pastor and staff to multiply their own gifts while encouraging others to develop their gifts from God. The equipping ministry includes motivating, encouraging, and preparing people for effective service in the body of Christ.

## Preaching

The minister is often called *preacher* because of his central task of communicating the gospel to people who gather for worship. It appears that there has been a resurgence of emphasis on dynamic preaching in Roman Catholicism as well as in Protestant and Evangelical churches during the past couple of decades. Prior to that time commentators on the pastoral situation seemed to unite in assuming that the pulpit had lost relevance and meaning in a world exposed to millions of words every week. Almost four decades ago, Russell Dicks summarized a chapter on preaching and pastoral care with the declaration that "preaching as the most effective method of carrying on the work of the Kingdom has turned the corner. . . . I have this further feeling, men and women with a fair amount of intelligence can be taught how to avoid doing harm in pastoral work, while no amount of instruction can teach them how to avoid doing harm through preaching."[2]

Contrary to Dick's melancholy comment, preaching is being re-emphasized rather than deemphasized in contemporary theological education. John Killinger, a well-known pastor and former professor of preaching, captures this interest in his book *The Centrality of Preaching in the Total Task of the Ministry*. Believing that the preaching task can become a center for ordering the minister's life and study, Killinger encourages the preacher to "set the business of preaching at the very center of your life and work, and give it first claim on your time and energy." Killinger's recommendation may seem to be in conflict with Wynn's advice to organize pastoral work around family ministry but that need not be true. "To speak thus of the primacy of preaching is not to say that preaching is in any way independent of pastoral care," declared Killinger. "On the contrary, there is a vital relationship between the two."[3] Authentic preaching is needed that is pastorally focused and deals with the crises in family living that confront today's parishioners.

Pastoral preaching is an outgrowth of a person-centered ministry. One of the earliest advocates of life-situation preaching, as this approach came to be described, was Harry Emerson Fosdick at the Riverside Baptist Church in New York City. In 1928 Fosdick criticized the preaching of his contemporaries because it lacked contact with the realities of life. He maintained that "every sermon should have for its main business the solving of some problem" because "preaching is wrestling with individuals over questions of life and death, and until that idea of it commands a preacher's mind and method, eloquence will avail him little and theology not at all."[4] Even though I would not agree that *every* sermon should be a life-situation type, I concur that such preaching is one of the essential means of communicating the gospel to the person in the pew.

Pastoral preaching is also a form of group counseling since it is through preaching that the pastor is able to deal on a group basis with many of the problems experienced by members of the church and those with whom he comes in contact outside of the membership. The persistence of common problems among church attenders can be seen by comparing survey results quoted by Edgar N. Jackson in 1956 with a 1978 survey. Of the four thousand respondents in 1956, almost half felt the major problems of their lives to be personal matters, such as "futility, insecurity, loneliness, marriage problems, sex, alcoholism, false ideas about religion and morals, inferiority, suffering, illness, frustration and guilt feelings. Nearly a quarter of the persons were concerned about family problems, child training, infidelity, separation, divorce, poor adjustment to marriage, symptoms of personal problems as they touch the lives of others."[5] The 1978 Southern Baptist sampling of 426 persons including pastors and married couples revealed similar family concerns. Among the top ten family problems were family communication, discipline of children, conflict resolution, money management, handling negative emotions such as anger, expression of affection, and decision-making in the home.[6]

When a pastor speaks to the problems indicated in the preceding lists and shows a helpful attitude toward individuals caught up in these problems, he will discover that his preaching actually becomes a preparation for counseling. Killinger maintained that "the sermon ought always to constitute a pre-counseling situation, and prepare the way for the most effective personal confrontation between the minister and the counselee."[7] The rigid, authoritarian proclaimer who is unmoved by the heartbreak of humanity is not apt to have many personal interviews. The pastor who truly speaks as a shepherd to the flock will be kept busy helping troubled people face life's problems.

The foregoing statements are not to be understood as advocating that the pulpit become a substitute for the psychiatrist's couch. The preacher should never forget that he speaks as an interpreter of the revelation of God rather than as an amateur psychologist. His preaching is not merely sanctified psychology. It must clearly and forcefully present God's judgment on the sin and complacency of our modern world yet do this in a way that identifies the preacher and congregation together in their desire to become what God intends for them to be. The principles of psychology are needed and helpful, but the declaration of God's grace in forgiveness and healing must always remain central in the preacher's response to human hurt.

It is obvious from the research that family needs are a focal point for pastoral preaching. My own experience in church-sponsored family enrichment programs has proven forcefully that Christian people are anxious for help from the minister in these vital areas of daily concern. Unfortunately, however, many pastors do not seize the opportunity for constructive pulpit counseling. For example, only 25 percent of the 192 pastors responding to the SBC survey reported preaching family related sermons as a part of the church's response to felt needs. I want to suggest four specific objectives for pastoral preaching on the family that are needed today.

1. *Interpreting the biblical-theological concepts of selfhood, marriage, and family living to the congregation.* Popular psychologies and newspaper columnists may have more influence on church members' understanding of self-identity and marriage than do our churches because of our neglect to teach them. For example, in the specific area of sexuality, there is an abundance of literature discussing it solely in terms of biological and psychological implications. For the Christian faith, however, human sexuality does not find its meaning solely in the human context but includes the intention and purpose of God for sex.

Sexuality, therefore, can never be dealt with apart from the biblical-theological rootage we have in the Bible. Experiences with youth and adults suggest that they seldom have been made aware of the relationship between sex and Christian faith in any positive and meaningful way. In a survey which I conducted in cooperation with the Family Ministry Department of The Sunday School Board of the Southern Baptist Convention over one-third of the nonpastoral respondents indicated a desire for the pastor to include sermons on Christian sex education in his pulpit ministry. This is only one example of the need for preaching that relates the basic theological affirmations of the Christian faith to family experience.

2. *Centering the interpersonal relations of the family in a context of redemptive love and forgiveness.* Love and forgiveness are essential to the development of personal relationships in the home. When we remember that a family is a world in miniature which encompasses all the kinds of conflict that life continually faces, we realize that it will not endure

without the willingness to give and receive love and forgiveness. Kenneth Chafin highlights a common myth about families in the persistent belief of some people that normal Christian families do not experience stress in their interpersonal relationships. He points out that "this myth remains despite the fact that every significant study of the family demonstrates the normal family does not always live in perfect harmony, does get ruffled at times, and does not always cooperate with one another. The difference between the healthy and the destructive family is not the absence of problems but how those problems are seen and dealt with."[8]

The Christian faith offers a significant dimension to these interpersonal relationships of the family. Because Christianity centers its own theology in an event of love which provides forgiveness for sin and failure, Christian faith offers to the family a possibility of love which redeems the home through forgiveness and inspiration for life.

3. *Offering constructive guidance in the common life challenges of family relationships.* Reference was made in chapter 1 to the family life cycle and to developmental stages of human experience. In his preaching ministry, the pastor will seek to relate the meaning of the gospel and the teachings of the church to the common problems involved in the life cycle. This includes what Elton Trueblood calls the common life ventures of birth, death, marriage, and work. It certainly will mean that the pastor will speak to the specific problems that people bring to him, to the relationships between husbands and wives, parents and children, and to the developmental aspects of the individual's life as it is lived within the context of the family.

John Claypool illustrates beautifully the art of preaching on the common life ventures as reflected in his books *Stages* and *Tracks of a Fellow Struggler. Stages,* subtitled *The Art of Living the Expected,* contains four sermons focused on childhood, adolescence, adulthood, and senior adulthood. These were first preached in a month-long emphasis on "The Saga of Life" at Broadway Baptist Church, Fort Worth, Texas. Claypool used David as the central character in the sermons. His desire in the sermons was to "blend the light of biblical wisdom with the best from the behavioral sciences."[9] In his other book, Claypool reflects upon the grief struggle he and his family faced in the death of his ten-year-old daughter by leukemia.

4. *Declaring redemptive hope to persons whose marriages have failed.* Since over one million marriages end in divorce each year in the United States, virtually every pastor will preach to divorced persons in his congregation at some time. The nature of that message will vary from church to church, but the situation provides an opportunity for the divorced to hear a needed word of renewal and hope.

The lady lingered after the evening service of a family life conference to speak to me. "I am amazed at what I heard tonight," she declared. "All my life in the church I have heard that divorce is virtually unforgivable, but here tonight you have preached on the possibility of forgiveness and a new beginning for people who have been divorced. You may wonder why this has affected me so deeply, but you see, I have spent the day in the courthouse across the street being divorced by my husband of eighteen years."

The tiredness of the day revealed itself in her face as she continued, "My friends told me that I should come to this family conference, but I did not want to do so. I felt I would be hearing all about ideal families, and I couldn't stand that! But your message tonight has helped me to look forward to beginning again, and I thank you for it."

The preaching role of the minister is without parallel as an opportunity to encourage family ministry and to help families apply the teachings of faith to everyday life. This is one of the most significant influences on a church's acceptance of family ministry as a responsibility for service to itself and its community.

### Participating

In addition to being a motivator, equipper, and preacher, the minister can also encourage congregational participation in family-related programs by personal involvement in them. This suggestion calls in question the minister's own view of his relationship to members of the congregation and to his role in leadership. The model of pastoral leadership which emphasizes the necessity for the minister to remain aloof from the congregation in personal areas in order to maintain a leadership role would discourage the minister's participation in groups where personal sharing is expected unless the minister is the group leader. As leader the minister can encourage others to share personal family experiences but can avoid sharing his own.

If the minister sees his identity with the congregation as more peer-related, the minister and spouse may become coparticipants in family enrichment experiences along with members of the congregation. I have conducted marriage enrichment retreats in which staff members and their spouses were able to be group participants along with church members in such an open manner that the church members experienced a new sense of relatedness to the ministers.

One of these pastors was sharing his own experience of the marriage enrichment retreat with a family enrichment conference group. After describing feelings of initial hesitancy that he and his wife had, he told the group how much it had helped his own marriage for the two of them to grapple with personal issues along with couples from his church. Rather humorously he said, "As we came to the last exercise of the retreat, I was feeling pretty good about the picture I had given to the group of the husband that I was. But then that meek sweet little wife of mine really let me have it right there in front of everybody as the group dealt with changes we would like to see in our marriage! In fact, after the retreat, we stopped at a grocery store to pick up a few things and spent over an hour in the parking lot discussing our marriage." As a result of the retreat, church members understood the humanity of their minister more fully but did not lose their respect for him as a spiritual leader for all of them.

Obviously the minister or staff members will not be available to participate in all family-related activities. The equipping function requires that the minister encourage and help others to carry on that responsibility. It is true, however, that personal participation by the professional staff gives greater importance to the activities in the thinking of lay people. In addition, the minister's own marriage and family can be nurtured by participating in these programs along with other church families.

Dale Keeton, minister of counseling of the Columbia Baptist Church in Falls Church, Virginia, highlighted this fact in his address to the Southern Baptist Christian Life Commission Seminar on Strengthening Families in 1982. After he and his wife became certified instructors in the Couple Communication Program, they offered this course to church members whose marriages were not in difficulty. Keeton pointed out that it was difficult to communicate this need to couples who were not currently hurting until the pastor and his wife took the course and began to promote it from their own experience.

These are strategic roles for ministers in developing a perspective on family ministry in the church through their personal support and participation. In fulfilling family life education goals, there needs also to be an appropriate perspective on the nature of the tasks itself. In this book two basic approaches to meeting family needs will be described—education and ministry.

### Educational Task

One aspect of the church's family focus is to educate people for more effective living in families. Teaching was central in the life of Christ as he lived among the people, and one of his last instructions to the disciples was to teach new converts "to observe all that I have commanded you" (Matt. 28:20). The apostle Paul, along with Barnabas, went to Antioch where "for a whole year they met with the church, and taught a large company of people" (Acts 11:26). Paul's insistent instruction to Timothy was "command and teach these things" (1 Tim. 4:11). Education in the gospel and Christian life has been a constant responsibility for the church ever since it began. Therefore, to maintain that the church has an educational task in family living is to affirm one specific application of its traditional role.

### Developmental

In the fulfillment of its educational opportunity, the basic purpose is to help persons realize the fullness of Christian family life throughout the life cycle of the family and in the developmental stages of personal life. Each stage is not a separate compartment but is a transitional time in which new developmental tasks must be handled. These tasks grow out of the changing needs of the family members along with changing expectations of the society for successful family life. Satisfactory accomplishment of these developmental tasks is based upon physical, social, psychological, and spiritual growth and yields a sense of personal happiness and competence in family living.

The terms *accomplishment* and *competence* are carefully chosen. They connote functional application of what they have learned in actual life situations, and this is essential to the educational task. Several years ago David R. Mace, internationally recognized family life specialist, described education for marriage as an ineffective remedy for the crisis confronting marriage in our country. His reasoning was that providing information is not in itself a significant means for bringing about behavioral or relational change. Willingness or determination to change demands more than exposure to good information.

Mace concluded, therefore, that behavioral change required two factors in addition to new information. One is "*insight,* which interprets information to enable us to explain and understand our own functioning," and the other is "*action,* which is necessary before insight can be put to use."[10]

Competence refers to the development of skills necessary for successful accomplishment of tasks. In reference to family life, it means developing the skills necessary for understanding the interactions between people and learning better ways of relating to each other. Competence, therefore, includes the use of insight into self and others within an experiential situation that provides an opportunity to accomplish new relationships.

A marriage enrichment retreat is one illustration of an educational activity designed for learning through experience rather than solely by exposure to new data about marriage. A candidate for the Doctor of Ministry degree at Midwestern Baptist Theological Seminary developed a proposal for a marriage enrichment project which included a retreat. He was angered when his committee insisted that his retreat model was too cognitive and not experiential enough. He reluctantly altered his plan at the committee's urging since he still believed that marriages can be changed by new information. Only after his program was in process and he had led several marriage enrichment retreats could he acknowledge that couples must act as well as study for behavior to change. This insight is vitally important to churches as they plan educational opportunities for personal growth.

## Preventive

A second component of the educational task is that it is essentially preventive in purpose. Even though at times educational approaches attempt to remedy existing problems, the fundamental assumption is that difficulties may be prevented or made less threatening by educational preparation before they occur.

Conflict resolution in marriage may be used to illustrate the preventive focus of education. Surveys report that many Christian couples have difficulty dealing constructively with conflict between themselves. In my own recent research, 28 percent of the couples and 20 percent of the pastors acknowledged that they did not have satisfactory patterns of conflict resolution.

In some cases the couples were unwilling to admit anger and rejection because they did not believe Christians should "be like that." Their churches had not helped them understand anger as a normal ingredient in family life; therefore, they were not helped to anticipate differences and learn to resolve them. Experiential educational opportunities exploring biblical and psychological insights into anger resolution could help them prevent destructive blowups through appropriate understanding and behavior. This can be described as preventive education when the church enters into this kind of marriage preparation.

The educational task may be accomplished through the regular Sunday activities of study and training, through conferences and seminars on selected family issues, through marriage and family enrichment programs and retreats, through workshops on parenting, and through growth groups for couples and families. It is a responsibility for which the church is ideally suited if the willingness to do so is present.

## Ministry Opportunities

Thus far the term *ministry* has been used in two basic ways. Family *ministry* is the total program of support given to families through all of the church's resources. *Ministry* has also been defined as a helping response to humanity's hurt and search for wholeness. This second definition will be explored in the consideration of ministry opportunities both inside and outside of the church family. This phase of family ministry is both interventional and remedial.

### Interventional

Pastor John Switzer of the Hillcrest Methodist Church became concerned about the Jacobsen family in his congregation. They had been absent from the church services which they normally attended, and he had been getting some feedback from their friends that the marriage might be in trouble. After waiting some time to see if the couple would approach him about their difficulties, he decided to call on them and offer his help.

George and June Jacobsen were both home when he called. After a few minutes of discussion about their absence from church, the pastor said, "I have been concerned about your church attendance, but I am more concerned that you may be struggling with some family problems that are making things difficult for you. Reports which have come to me may not be true; but if they are, I want you to know of my concern and my availability to help if I can."

George glanced quickly at June before replying. "Well, Pastor, I guess our friends have talked to you because they care about us. Yes, June and I have been struggling with a pretty serious conflict between us, and this has made it difficult for us to come to church. I appreciate your willingness to help us, and I think June will join me in accepting your help."

One of the great assets of the church for ministry to human need is the general acceptability for intervention into situations even before help is requested. In the crises of death, illness, divorce, job loss, problems with children, and many other such critical problems, church folk can offer help that may ease the stress of the crisis.

A word of caution is necessary however. Ministry to persons cannot be effectively fulfilled without the person's desire or consent to accept such help. The minister or church member may intervene but be rebuffed if the person is not ready for help. A pastor calling on one of his parishioners in the hospital knew that the woman and her husband were having marital problems. In response to his inquiry about how things were going at home, she quickly snapped back, "Just fine! Just fine!" She was not ready to accept his invitation to open the door on her home problems even though she appreciated his visit to her in the hospital.

### Remedial

Whereas education was described as primarily preventive, ministry is most often remedial. It deals with family situations which are already caught up in stress of some kind. Helping a church member cope with the reality of divorce is illustrative of the remedial ministry of the whole church. Personal counseling with the minister could help deal with the grief process of a broken marriage, but congregational care and acceptance are often important to the healing of brokenness. Friends and other support persons are needed during the transition period for the husband and wife. Children face unusual tensions when parents divorce. They need the supportive help of persons who can hear their struggle and provide an outlet for anger and fear.

The family of God in the church has the wonderful opportunity of being ministers to the hurt and rejection which people in difficulty experience. Unfortunately this healing expression of grace may become lost in the human tendency to be critical rather than redemptive. This may be especially true when the crisis involves some form of moral transgression or even in case of divorce. Peter's question to Jesus and our Lord's answer put our problem of unforgiveness in sharp focus.

"'Lord, how often shall my brother sin against me, and I forgive him?

As many as seven times?' Jesus said to him, 'I do not say to you seven times, but seventy times seven'" (Matt. 18:21-22).

Then Jesus told the story about a servant who was forgiven of a great debt when he cried out for mercy from his creditor. The same man, however, refused to forgive the debt of one who owed him a small sum. He refused to grant to another the grace which he himself had received. When the creditor heard of it, he had the unforgiving debtor thrown into jail until he could pay all he owed. Jesus then applied the parable to other relationships when he said, "So also my heavenly Father will do to every one of you, if you do not forgive your brother from your heart" (Matt. 18:35).

The healing ministry of the church offers forgiveness and renewal, as well as food, shelter, friendship, and a listening ear. With so many families struggling against economic, social, and emotional pressures, remedial ministry is desperately needed by many folk.

We are now ready to investigate specific programs that churches may use to accomplish some of the objectives discussed in these first three chapters. We will begin with personhood development in chapter 4, move to marriage in chapter 5, and deal with family relationships in chapter 6. These three chapters are primarily related to the educational task of the church, even though remedial ministry is also involved. Chapter 7 will focus on ministry to family needs, and chapter 8 will suggest guidelines for developing a total family life program.

# 4
# Preparing Persons for Maturing Adulthood

I am convinced that the New Testament is growth-oriented! God accepts us and renews us at whatever stage of life we respond to his love, but he does not intend for us to remain children in faith and experience. Growth is expected but it does not happen automatically. I like John Ishee's comment that a "person must decide to grow. It takes effort. God gives the increase when this effort is put forth."[1]

Jesus expected his followers to grow. In the Sermon on the Mount, he informed his disciples that they were to "be perfect, as your heavenly Father is perfect" (Matt. 5:48). The maturity of character reflected in the teachings of the sermon is the goal for the new selfhood in Christ, particularly as described in the Beatitudes (Matt. 5:2-12). We will never achieve perfection in this life, but the challenge of growing toward it gives excitement to daily experience.

Paul's Letter to the Ephesians also emphasized the growth principle. After the believer finds salvation by faith (2:8-10), the Christian life is to be one of continual growth. Paul maintained that "speaking the truth in love, we are to grow up in every way unto him who is the head, into Christ" (4:15). The developmental principle of moving from immature faith to mature faith is one emphasis in Paul's writing for growth toward maturity as a person.

The writer of Hebrews spoke in similar fashion. After rebuking his Christian hearers for lack of growth in faith, he declared:

> You have become people who need a milk diet and cannot face solid food! For anyone who continues to live on "milk" is unable to digest what is right—he simply has not grown up. "Solid food" is only for the adult, that

is, for the man who has developed by experience his power to discrimi-
nate between what is good and what is evil. Let us leave behind the
elementary teaching about Christ and go forward to adult understanding"
(Heb. 5:12-6:1, Phillips).

Even though the focus of this passage is on doctrinal maturity, the
emphasis on growth toward maturity is clearly evident.

Churches are challenged to examine their theology and educational
principles in light of the opportunity to help persons become maturing
adults. In this task, we face the basic needs of children, youth, and
adults for helpful insights into their self-concept, sexuality, friendships,
and ultimate choices about singleness or marriage.

### Developing a Healthy Christian Self-Concept

"All the problems facing the church will find healing answers if we
start with and do not get distracted at any time from meeting every
person's deepest need—his hunger for self-esteem, self-worth and
personal dignity." So affirms Dr. Robert Schuller, minister of the Crystal
Cathedral, Garden Grove, California, in his challenging book *Self-
Esteem: The New Reformation.*[2] Schuller is convinced that the human
desire for self-esteem is fundamental to all other needs of the person and
argues forcefully for the church to give more attention in its theology
and teachings to that common heart-hunger of humanity.

While writing the book, Schuller commissioned George Gallup, Jr., of
the Gallup poll fame, to investigate the self-esteem of the American
public. Persons who described themselves in positive self-esteem terms
were found to "demonstrate the qualities of personal character that the
church would happily point to with pride in the members that we
develop within our institutions."[3] The research revealed, however, that a
minority of Christian believers had this kind of positive self-esteem.
Without citing actual research data, Schuller declared that only 35
percent of the Protestants, 39 percent of Catholics, and 40 percent of
persons in "other faiths" demonstrated a strong self-esteem. Thus,
concluded Schuller, the church is "missing the mark" in its ministry to
its own members as well as to the society.

Without committing oneself to all that Schuller defends in his book, the research findings by Gallup are supported by other interpreters of the contemporary scene. On an incomplete sentence form used by one Christian counseling center, the question appears, "When I look in the mirror I see. . . ." Answers given are quite revealing about some people's sense of personhood or self-identity.

One woman wrote, "I see a careless housewife with mixed emotions." A man saw "some things I would change in myself." A divorcee described a "failure as a mate." In each of these cases, the individuals were disturbed about relationships to a wife, husband, or other family members. Their image of themselves, therefore, was affected by the conflict in their lives. The mirror simply reflected back their loss of self-esteem based on their sense of disappointment and failure.

The struggle to know and understand one's personhood or selfhood is not limited to persons in emotional stress nor is it limited to adults. Children and young people also express their need to be affirmed as individual persons and to gain a better understanding of their selfhood. The experience of a Missouri pastor with his three children—an eight-year-old girl and four-year-old twins—is illustrative of the concern about self that children may feel.

His church was engaged in a weekend family enrichment conference. During the first session on Friday evening, the importance of a positive self-concept as one important contribution of a fulfilling family experience was stressed. When the service was over, the pastor took his three children home while his wife visited with another family in the church. Arriving home, the children and father talked about their experience at the church that evening.

Then the eight-year-old, who had been in the conference session with her parents, told her father that she did not really like herself. Surprised by this confession, he tried to reassure her about how much he liked her just as she was and then he encouraged the twins to tell their sister what they liked about her. This discussion continued for a few minutes before dad got another shock. The four-year-old girl told her father that she thought he might like the male twin better than he did her. When asked why she felt this way, she replied, "Because he was born first, and I wasn't sure you really wanted two!"

As the pastor-father shared this experience at the men's fellowship breakfast the next morning, he told them he had no idea that his young children had such negative thoughts about themselves. He said that all four of them ended up crying and affirming how much they really liked each other as bedtime came for the children.

In another situation, thirteen-year-old Jennifer wrote: "The other night I lay awake wondering. Who am I? What purpose do I serve in life? What am I like? Am I really me? I thought about it, and I discovered that when you're my age you can't really answer those questions. People say, 'Be yourself!' But I don't know who I am."[4]

Probably each of these individuals could identify with Paul when he wrote, "At present we are men looking at puzzling reflections in a mirror," and would long to believe that "the time will come when we shall see reality whole and face to face!" (1 Cor. 13:12, Phillips). This search for honesty, for reality, for acceptance is certainly one human need that churches can hear and respond to in our society today. In order to do so, we must examine our theology and our educational programming.

### Christian Faith and Selfhood

Within the biblical setting, selfhood or personhood is described in at least three ways. The first is suggested by the creation of human life in the "image of God" (Gen. 1:26-27; see 5:1-2). Here man and woman are pictured as bearing in their personality the authentic nature of God in a manner similar to that of a child bearing the genetic inheritance of its parents. God as the Supreme Person—free, wise, loving—breathes into his creation the breath of life and makes them persons able to respond in devotion to their Creator and in joy to one another (Gen. 2:23-25).

Translations of the Bible often use the term *man* to refer to both male and female rather than simply to male as can be seen in Genesis 5:1-2: "When God created man, he made him in the likeness of God. Male and female he created them, and he blessed them and named them Man when they were created." Thus we see the psalmist marveling at God's handiwork of creation as he asks wonderingly, "What is man that thou art mindful of him,/and the son of man that thou dost care for him?/Yet thou hast made him a little less than God,/and dost crown him with glory and honor" (Ps. 8:4-5).

Even Job, in the fury of his argument with God because of his unexplained torment, reflected an awareness of the glory that is in human life because of God's loving concern: "What is man, that thou dost make so much of him,/and that thou dost set thy mind upon him,/dost visit him every morning, and test his every moment?" (7:17-18).

God created man and woman to be responsible persons in relationship to God, to self, to each other, and in their dominion over the natural world in which they lived. However, this potentiality for responsible personhood included the possibility of misusing God's gifts as well as rightfully using them. Thus the second picture which we have of man and woman in the Bible shows them rebelling against the Creator's purpose and consequently bringing upon themselves the experience of separation from God, from their better selves, and from each other (Gen. 3:1-12). This feeling of separation, or what is often called alienation, is vividly pictured by the biblical writer in his description of their attempt to cover their bodies with fig leaves and to hide from God among the trees. Their potential for growth was stunted by the reality of sin.

What can we say of self-worth in the light of the fall? Does a human being still possess worth even though living in separation from the Father? How a minister or church answers this question will significantly affect their ministry to persons in society. If the consequence of sin in its biblical portrayal is understood to mean that a person separated from God is worthless even from babyhood, then no human being can have worth before God and certainly cannot have self-worth. On the other hand, if sin in human experience means that all of one's life is touched by sin but the person still has worth to God, then self-worth is possible even in the fallen state. This does not mean that selfhood in the fullest meaning of God's redemptive love is possible apart from salvation through Christ, but it does mean that persons out of fellowship with God can still have worth as persons.

In the New Testament, the self thus separated from God's presence and purpose is called the "old self." Paul declared, "We know that our old self was crucified with him [Christ]" (Rom. 6:6) and in many vivid ways he described the nature of the old self. This person is separated from God's redemptive love in Christ, alienated from the community of faith within which growth toward maturity could take place, subject to the idolatry of self-worship, and is an enemy to the ultimate wholeness which God planned for human life (cf. Rom. 6; Eph. 2:1-12). Since this is a description of human misuse of one's potential, it is described as the sin of missing the mark of life which was intended by the Creator. Where is man's worth in light of these portraits of experience?

Essentially biblical interpreters maintain that human worth is shown precisely by the way in which the Father deals with the sin problem of human beings. He did not turn away in disgust from them, nor did he abandon them to their separation without providing a means of reconciliation. The Bible describes the old self as *helpless,* not *worthless*: "While we were still weak, at the right time Christ died for the ungodly" (Rom. 5:6). True worth is found in the way God cares for the separated. John expressed it clearly when he declared that "God so loved the world" (John 3:16). The old self is the object of God's redeeming love.

The third picture which we find in the Bible is that of the "new self" in contrast to the "old self." The translators of *The New English Bible* provide a helpful interpretation of the new selfhood in Christ in their rendering of Matthew 16:24-26. After Jesus had warned his disciples of his coming death in Jerusalem, he said to them:

> "If anyone wishes to be a follower of mine, he must leave self behind; he must take up his cross and come with me. Whoever cares for his own safety is lost; but if a man will let himself be lost for my sake, he will find his true self. What will a man gain by winning the whole world at the cost of his true self? Or what can he give that will buy that self back?"

Just as Paul and other New Testament writers vividly described the nature of the old self, so they give insight into the nature of this new or true self. This person is adopted into the family of God in love, sins of rebellion and missing the mark are forgiven and blotted out, there is participation in the fellowship of faith with other believers, and life is discovered that has meaning and purpose. Life is seen against the backdrop of eternity rather than the limited horizons of material goals and comforts. Although not freed from the problems of living in the proving ground of one's former environment, the new self can draw upon the resources of God and the faith community for strength to face trials and problems. The new self is a person whose relationships can be honest and authentic through willingness to open the heart to God and to others in ever-expanding love.

How does all this happen? The New Testament is clear and positive on this point—an individual discovers this true self through acceptance of and commitment to Jesus Christ as Savior and Lord. The self has its origin in the personality of God and realizes its most complete fulfillment through faith in Jesus Christ. Roy Honeycutt expressed this relationship beautifully in describing the human awakening to God's design for true selfhood in creation: "As soon as he feels the stirring of God's breath within; at that precise moment when he sees himself as made in the image of God, then it is that he inevitably begins to see himself as more than an animal. He sees himself as a person, created by God for true selfhood and dominion."[5] This occurs in the conversion experience of new birth just as it happened in the understanding of Adam and Eve as reflected in Genesis.

"But isn't self-centeredness the sin that caused human separation?" asked a pastor during a conference discussing selfhood. "Don't we make people feel that they are OK when we say that the unsaved have worth as persons?"

Yes, this pastor was exactly right in describing a basic fact of the fall and also suggesting his concern about the non-believer who is satisfied with self apart from God. However, the answer to his dilemma is not to stress more vehemently the worthlessness of life apart from God but to emphasize more clearly and forcefully the value of life in Christ. Jesus was clear on the fact that the self may be destroyed by self-centeredness and selfishness, but it is developed through self-denial. The seemingly contradictory fact that self-denial and self-development go hand in hand can only be approached from the heart of the Christian gospel. The denial of self-centeredness does not mean negating or rejecting the selfhood of the person. The stronger the self-concept, the more creatively can a person chose to reject selfishness and affirm self-giving in a humble response to the unconditional love of the Creator. Schuller is certainly right when he points out that "to be accepted and loved by the noblest of all persons really releases us from a negative self-image! Now we are able to forgive ourselves, and we are motivated to forgive others. We stop putting them down and start building them up!"[6]

The new self in Christ is forgiven but not perfect, renewed but not completed, redeemed but growing toward maturity. This concept is foundational to much that we will be discussing in the remaining portions of the book. Maturity is not a state of existence; it is a direction in life. Growing toward maturity is enhanced by an experiential conviction of living in the full acceptance of God's grace which continues to shape one's life toward the wholeness of personhood modeled by Jesus Christ. That conviction is fundamental in helping others share the same pilgrimage of growth through the ministry of the church.

## Self-Concept Formation

During recent years, an intense interest in personality theories concerning the self has developed among psychologists, especially those who specialize in the fields of social psychology and counseling. This concern which is central to person-centered psychology has become more dominant among Christian psychologists. Space prohibits any extended discussion of various contributions to these studies, but it is necessary to look briefly at a model of selfhood which is prominent among these scholars and therapists.

First, the person is a conscious or real self. This involves a conscious awareness of who one is and includes awareness of strengths, weaknesses, and the possibilities in the midst of the real world of human relationships. Some psychologists call this the phenomenal self since it is as real to the individual as are other phenomena in life—job, home, nature, and the material goods which support life.

Paul reflected a conscious awareness of his real self in his declaration, "I do not understand my own actions. For I do not do what I want, but I do the very thing I hate. For I do not do the good I want, but the evil I do not want is what I do" (Rom. 7:15,19). He was puzzled by his own inability, and this led to his understanding of God's great grace in Christ through whom he could find a new power for living. Each of us has a conscious self which can be known by others only as we are willing to reveal that self through some form of communication.

Second, the person is a public self. We present to others forms of behavior which will build an image in their minds of what we want them to think about us. A man naturally presents one image of himself to his wife and family, another to the people with whom he works, perhaps another to the foursome on the golf course, and yet another to his Sunday School class. Even though we all do this to some degree, the danger is that "our public selves become so estranged from our real selves that the net consequence is self-alienation; we no longer know our real selves."[7] Wearing masks may be fun at masquerade parties, but if we must always readjust our masks for every phase of total living we can lose our own identities in the desperate attempts to play the right parts.

Third, the person has an ideal self. The ideal self is what we would like to be. It includes motivations and goals for life which may be accurate or distorted, attainable or unattainable, reasonable or fanciful but offering some challenge to the meaning of our selfhood. This ideal model for our own life goals may have developed from paternal ideals, religious ideals, or other contacts which we experience in growing toward maturity.

Since our self-concept includes all of these dimensions, it is obvious that it has both content and feeling components. My self-concept is an object to me, but it is also a subject for me. It is this feeling or evaluation aspect of self-concept that is described as *self-esteem*. My positive feelings about myself are influenced by how closely my conscious self and public self are in agreement with my ideal self, and my negative self-rejection by how much I believe that I have failed to become my ideal self.

Human behavior often falls short of the ideal we expect of ourselves, thus it is easy to see why many people have negative images of themselves. If the ideal is measured against the standard of biblical expectations for personal life, failure is virtually guaranteed unless the new self has a clear awareness of the meaning of God's grace. Our theology must stress more positively the unconditional love of God for persons who seek to grow in Christ and not continually highlight their failure to be what we want to be. Paul found his answer in grace, and so must we!

Against the backdrop of this discussion of selfhood in theology and psychology, let us now discuss some ways that the churches can help in positive self-concept formation with children, youth, and adults.

## Self-Concept Development in Children

When young children are asked to describe themselves, the influence of their parents' definitions of them often can be seen in the results. Their self-concept is already being formed in response to their perceptions of how their parents feel about them. Even if these perceptions are wrong, they still influence the child's self-concept. The parents or parent substitutes are primary in their influence on the child's self-perception.

Since this is true, the church has its first opportunity to affect the child's self-concept by helping parents understand the important contribution they make to their children's self-image. Pediatrician W. Wayne Grant affirms this parental role in his response to the question, "What do I want for my children, anyway?" His answer, "I have come to believe that most of all we should want our children to develop that balanced sense of self-worth which allows them to respect themselves as well as others."[8]

One approach to accomplishing this objective is the STEP program published by the American Guidance Service.[9] Written by Don

Dinkmeyer and Gary D. McKay, Systematic Training for Effective Parenting assumes that all behavior has a social purpose and that parents can be trained to recognize the purposes underlying their children's behavior in order to appropriately guide it. The material includes a recorded introduction to the program, publicity resources for promoting it in the church, a handbook for parents which contains the essence of the teaching materials, a leader's manual for the teachers, five audio cassettes, and other supplementary resources.

This program is in harmony with Christian teachings, although not written as a Christian teaching tool. Leaders may apply the biblical concepts which will relate the teaching model more closely to Christian faith.

Another possibility is the use of Growing Parents Growing Children as a discussion resource for parents. Dr. Grant is a Southern Baptist who wrote the book as a component of that denomination's training program. Teaching procedures and bibliographic resources are included in the text. James Dobson's Hide or Seek is an excellent supplementary resource for this study. Churches can also use these resources to train persons working with children in their educational programs.

## Self-Concept Development in Youth

Psychologist Erik H. Erikson labels the adolescent period of life as the time when young people must cope with the crisis of identity versus role confusion. With the onset of puberty, childhood ends and youth begins. In adolescence "all samenesses and continuities relied on earlier are more or less questioned again, because of a rapidity of body growth which equals that of early childhood and because of the new addition of genital maturity."[10] Establishment of a positive self-concept during youth involves cutting the apron strings without losing one's family, achieving group acceptance without surrendering personal integrity, and adjusting to the demands of a changing body and new sexual feelings without being dominated by one's sexuality.

Churches can use youth retreats and camp experiences to focus on identity issues for youth. Getting away from the church setting seems to free youth for discussion and response more openly than in the educational building.

A helpful resource for group discussion among youth is the psychological perspective on human growth known as Transactional Analysis (TA). The concepts, language, and applications of TA are easily understandable for young people as they examine their own motivations for behavior and their development of an "I'm OK—You're OK" outlook on self and others. Major resources for leaders are *I'm OK—You're OK* by Thomas A. Harris, *Game Free* by Thomas Oden, and *Born to Love* by Muriel James. *Say Hello To Yourself* by Walter N. Wilson is written in TA language for young people. Exercises for group involvement included in the book can be used in church or retreat settings. While its specific source is from TA methodology, Wilson writes as a Christian interpreter of the program so as to relate it to the Christian faith.

## Self-Concept Development for Adults

"I have never felt that I had any real worth," declared a pastor's wife during a marriage enrichment retreat. Even though she was loved by her family and admired by her church, her self-esteem was very low. Through group discussion of her feelings, it became apparent that she had seldom received positive affirmation of her selfhood from her parents. Desperately wanting that support but seldom getting it made her feel unworthy. As an adult, the scars of her growing up years were still very real. Adults need to deal realistically with the adequacy of their own self-concept if they are going to be able to help their children become secure in their own self-identity.

Adults often center their self-identity in what they do rather than who they are. An exercise which can highlight this difference is to provide each adult in a conference or retreat setting a sheet of paper asking for two types of responses. At the top of the sheet is the caption "Who Am I?" with ten numbered lines below the heading for response. Participants are asked to write ten words or brief statements that identify themselves. After this has been done, they are invited to share their lists with the other group members. Attention can then be drawn by the group leader as to whether people identify themselves primarily by function or personhood. Group discussion of these contrasts can help individuals become more aware of the sources of their self-identity and can lead them to see their worth as persons in God's love.

The lower third of the page is used to write "Five Things I Like About Myself." While deceptively simple as an exercise in self-awareness, it challenges the person's sense of self-worth and self-acceptance. Many people discover that it is much easier to name ten things they don't like about themselves than to tell five things they do like! When this perspective is discussed in the group, it usually becomes apparent that these adults are confused about the meaning of pride, humility, and self-affirmation.

Craig Ellison, in *Your Better Self: Christianity, Psychology and Self-Esteem*, has a very helpful chart differentiating these concepts.[11] It can be used in the group to help them accept the right to feel good about self rather than to get caught up in a false humility which denies strengths while magnifying self-depreciation.

Comparison of True Humility, Pride, and False Humility

| True Humility | Pride | False Humility |
|---|---|---|
| 1. Based in self-worth. | 1. Based in self-doubt. | 1. Based in self-deprecation. |
| 2. Accepts both strengths and weaknesses. | 2. Denies weaknesses. | 2. Rejects strengths. |
| 3. Is open to both positive and negative feedback. | 3. Is closed to corrective and negative feedback. | 3. Is closed to affirmation and positive feedback. |
| 4. Results in accurate appraisal. | 4. Results in unrealistic appraisal (attitude of superiority). | 4. Results in unrealistic appraisal (attitude of inferiority). |

Transactional Analysis resources noted in the youth section are also applicable to adult conferences. When adults recognize how much their internalized images of themselves are often shaped by parental teachings and childhood feelings, changes in self-concept can result.

Self-concept formation based upon a positive theology and a Christian psychological perspective is a significant challenge in ministering to persons. It is fundamental to our next subject, education in human sexuality.

─────────────**Suggested Reading**─────────────

Brister, C. W. *Becoming You*. Rev. ed. Nashville: Broadman Press, 1980.
Fowler, James W. *Stages of Faith*. San Francisco: Harper and Row, 1981.
Jourard, Sidney. *The Transparent Self.* New York: Van Nostrand Reinhold 1971.
Tournier, Paul. *The Meaning of Persons*. New York: Harper and Row, 1957.

## Education for Responsible Sexuality

"Sex education in the church? Man, my people would have my job if I proposed some kind of sex education program for kids in our church!" Perhaps you identify with this exclamation by a pastor attending a workshop for family ministry in a Midwestern state. But is this statement really accurate? I determined to find out how church people in my own denomination might feel about this question while doing research on ethical issues facing families. The survey question was: "Should the church plan specific programs of sexual education in its educational planning?"

Of the 910 respondents to the survey, 35 did not answer the question (3.8 percent), 674 answered yes (74.1 percent), and 201 replied no (22.1 percent). The churches surveyed ranged from open country to large downtown churches with the range of membership being from approximately 300 to over 1500. In the open country, town, and small city categories, an average of 74.1 percent of the persons answering the questionnaire agreed that churches should include sexual education in their educational programming. The highest affirmative percentage was registered by the large downtown church members (88.9 percent) and the lowest percentage of agreement was from village churches (52.4 percent).

This data suggests that ministers who resist including sexual education planning in the church calendars may be so fearful of the minority that they neglect the majority who would welcome such activities. A further analysis of the data indicates that of the 309 pastors responding, 79.3 percent favor sex education in the church. Singles were strongly in favor (76 percent), remarried persons slightly less with 74.2 percent, whereas intact families dropped down to 67.7 percent in favor. You will note that even with the drop, over two-thirds of these families approved of sex education in the church.

For the church to enter into this type of education effectively, it must first clarify its own understanding of the purpose and nature of its sexual education program. Even though some people are convinced that sex education has a primary goal of preventing non-marital sexual intercourse and venereal disease, this is not true as an ultimate goal. A good sexual education *may* help decrease such sexual problems as premarital sex, unmarried pregnancies, and venereal disease. But this will concern only a portion of all the persons involved in the program. The major purpose of Christian sex education is to equip young people and adults to accept their own sexuality as a God-given force to be expressed in ways that will increase their sense of fulfillment in life as responsible persons. This will help them to be better prepared for living with their own sexual drives in growing up and will prepare them to be better sexual partners in marriage.

Confusion also exists about the nature of sex education. Parents and church leaders alike may be thinking in terms of sex *instruction* rather than sex *education*. Obviously the biological facts of sexual growth and reproduction are essential elements of sexual understanding, but this by itself is not sexual education. Rather, sex education is the continuous process of guiding young people and adults to develop and live with a set of values about sex and its place in human development in the light of these basic biological factors. In doing this, the developmental model of human growth is helpful for discussing ways to do sexual education.

## Developmental Opportunities

1. *Preadolescence.* In the period immediately preceding puberty, the church has an opportunity to use its educational organizations to help boys and girls get ready for the changes that will soon catapult them into

new ways of looking at their worlds of school, home, and church. The most helpful kind of sex education should precede the specific need for it but be close enough to that need to use the teachable moment to the best advantage. Of the survey respondents who favored sex education in churches, 21.6 percent believed that the best ages for beginning specific programming was between 6 and 10 years of age. This would begin earlier than puberty but would prepare the way for understanding the changes soon taking place in their bodies and feelings.

2. *Adolescence.* With the onset of menstruation for girls and the emission of semen for boys, adolescence becomes a condition of life rather than a concept to be studied! Dancing, dating, petting, drinking, smoking, drugs, and a host of other social invitations become challenging times of personal decision-making which force adolescents to rely upon their own moral resources in a multitude of decisions.

Since adolescence also crystallizes the child's struggle to become an independent self distinct from parents, the church can fulfill the very vital role of supplementing parental teachings through other responsible adults just when the youngsters feel the greatest need to rebel against parental authority. Over 40 percent of the survey respondents believed that between the ages of 11 and 14 was the best time to provide sex education opportunities. Of the persons favoring sex education methods, almost 70 percent felt that this best can be done through programs and retreats for youth with an emphasis on sexual development and dating relationships.

3. *Premarital Preparation.* As adolescence gives way to young adulthood and marriage preparation, the church shares a creative moment in helping to prepare its youth for courtship and marriage. Specific attention will be given to this responsibility later in the book, but at this time we recognize that sex education is part of that opportunity.

Sexual roles and attitudes need to be explored in groups where boys and girls can be involved together for study and interaction. They will learn much from each other that can create better and more responsible companionship in their dating relationships, as they understand more fully how sexual desire and pressure may affect them. Christian ethical values concerning sexuality can be studied as one phase of growing maturity in self-understanding and understanding of the opposite sex. Marital sexuality can be discussed to help them prepare for sex roles in marriage.

4. *Marital Sexuality.* Churches are giving greater attention to helping married couples develop a happier and more fulfilling sexual life through marriage enrichment retreats and through seminar or conference activities in the church setting. Even though this aspect of sexual education was favored by only 52.2 percent of the survey respondents, this figure still reflects a significant support for such programs.

5. *Parental Guidance.* The task comes full circle when these young adults become the sex educators of their own children. As the church has tried to instill in them healthy attitudes toward sex in its teaching program, it now has the responsibility of helping them educate their own children. Understandably, this phase of sex education programming has the greatest support from the constituency. Ninety percent of the respondents advocated programs for parents to help them provide sexual education for their children.

## Educational Models

Noland Road Baptist Church in Kansas City, Missouri, developed a four-day program to include guidance for parents as well as discussion of marital sexuality. Beginning on Sunday evening, two hours were used to discuss biblical and theological interpretations of human sexuality. Adults and youth were invited to this session and separate sessions on family were provided for younger children. Monday evening was devoted to parental training for sex education in the home; Tuesday evening was for junior and senior high youth; and Wednesday evening focused on marital sexual life. The discussion leader used audiovisual resources as well as introducing books for each age group to use at home. Church response was very positive in attendance and affirmation.

Leaders in the Park Baptist Church, Brookfield, Missouri, and the biology teacher in the local high school became concerned about the

*How to have a*

## *Happy Home*
### *without really trying*

**DON'T KID YOURSELF — IT CAN'T BE DONE!**
**BUT — You Can Strengthen Your Home By**
**Attending The**
**INSTITUTE OF CHRISTIAN FAMILY LIVING**
**PARK BAPTIST CHURCH**
**Brookfield, Missouri**

| Youth in Dialogue 6:30 p.m. | | Families at Worship 7:30 p.m. |
|---|---|---|
| GOD'S PURPOSES FOR SEX | Sept. 18 Howell | THE CHRISTIAN HOME IN A CHANGING AMERICA |
| THE STORY OF LIFE | Sept. 25 Howell | THE MIRACLE OF DIALOGUE |
| DATING QUESTIONS | Oct. 2 Hudson | FORGIVENESS IN FAMILY LIVING |
| IS IT LOVE? | Oct. 9 Howell | CONTRASTS IN LOVE |
| THE TEENAGER AND HIS PARENTS | Oct. 16 Hudson | CHRISTIAN DOCTRINE IN FAMILY LIVING |
| YOUTH'S COURTSHIP PROBLEMS | Oct. 23 Howell | CREATING HARMONY IN MARRIAGE |
| PLANNING A CHRISTIAN MARRIAGE | Oct. 30 Howell | CONFRONTING THE DIVORCE PROBLEM |

**SEPTEMBER 11    6:00 p.m. for Adults Only**
PREVIEW SESSION ON YOUTH DISCUSSION PROGRAMS
FOR PARENTS AND YOUTH LEADERS

## CONFERENCE LEADERS

DR. JOHN C. HOWELL

Professor of Christian Ethics
Midwestern Baptist Theological Seminary
Kansas City, Missouri

Member:
NATIONAL COUNCIL ON FAMILY RELATIONS

DR. R. LOFTON HUDSON

Director
Midwest Christian Counseling Center
Kansas City, Missouri

Member:
AMERICAN ASS'N of MARRIAGE COUNSELORS

number of high school girls becoming pregnant. Since there was no formal sex education program in the school, the church was asked to provide some type of program that could help the young people in the community to have a better understanding of sexual involvements in their dating life. The sheet included here was distributed to the high school youth as well as to homes of church members. The young people of the church invited other youth in the community to come, and the pastor of the Christian Church, which had no evening service, brought the youth from his church.

The young people were invited to the 6:30 activity, and no pressure was put on them to attend the worship services which were developed around family themes. Films and discussion guides were used with the youth, and cards for questions to be submitted to the leaders were made available each night. Between 100 and 125 young people attended each of the seven sessions. If such a program were being planned again, it would be profitable to include some time for a parent-youth dialogue, as well as having the sessions only for the youth.

Under the direction of Dorothy Russell, a community educator serving in the Mississippi County Family Planning organization, the First Methodist Church of Blytheville, Arkansas, conducted a six-week program using ministers, physicians, nurses, instructors from the local community college, and junior high teachers. The sessions, designed for junior highs and their parents, met for one hour each Sunday evening at the church and included joint, as well as separate, time for parents and youth. Attention was given to biological information, psychological insights on sexual development, sociological involvements of both parents and children, plus a strong emphasis on the spiritual meanings of sexuality. Participants rated the program highly and recommended that in future sessions more attention be given to values, responsibility, parent/child communication, and self-control of emotions.

A Georgia church decided to include sexual education in the regular Sunday morning Bible teaching time for junior and senior highs. The following table shows how they developed the teaching situation for the various age groups.

| Introduction | 7th | 8th | 9th | 10th | 11th | 12th |
|---|---|---|---|---|---|---|
| Interest in body knowledge assumed Questions invited Affirmation Biblical basis for sex as good Responsibility For use of sex and other gifts from God Forgiveness For failure to act responsibility in sexual matters Reproductive System Secondary Sex Characteristics Becoming a Man or Woman | 1½ hours annually to introduce all of these areas | 1½ hours annually to introduce all of these areas | 2 hours annually: 1 hour on the outlined material 1 hour for questions and discussion | 4 hours on alternate years | 4 hours on alternate years | 4 hours on alternate years |

The leaders found that line drawings on overhead transparencies was the simplest way to introduce body differences. Information on the Affirmation-Responsibility-Forgiveness approach was taken from Thomas E. Brown, *A Guide for Christian Sex Education of Youth.* Parents were informed about the program, but the young people were not required to have parental approval for participation.

## Developmental Resources

Several sets of books are available to assist parents give wholesome and accurate information to their children. The Concordia Education Series includes five books with accompanying color filmstrips and recorded narration. The parents' book, *Parents Guide to Christian*

*Conversation about Sex,* is keyed to the children's books. The youth book, *Life Can Be Sexual,* does not have an accompanying filmstrip, but it is discussed in the parents' guide.

Broadman Press has a similar series under the heading of "Sexuality in Christian Living" without the filmstrips. Included in the series are *Made to Grow* (6-8 year-olds), *The Changing Me* (9-11), *Growing Up With Sex* (junior high), *Sex Is More Than A Word* (senior high), and *Teaching Your Children About Sex* which I wrote for parents. An additional book in this series is for young adults entitled *Made For Each Other.*

Both of these series are produced by Christian denominational offices and include strong affirmations of biblical understandings of human sexuality. Budlong Press has an excellent series for the medical profession which is also available to ministers. The titles are *A Doctor Talks to 5-to-8 Year-Olds, A Doctor Talks to 9-12 Year-Olds, What Teenagers Want To Know,* and *Doctor's Marital Guide for Patients.* The book for 9-12s has a removable insert for parents to use when they give the book to their child. Although not written as Christian resources, these books are compatible with the Christian understanding of responsible sexual life.

These resources and others can be used by churches as textbooks for classes in Christian sexual education for parents. The parents' books have additional booklists and some recommended visual aids to use in such studies. Having parents role-play being children of various ages can test the ability of the parents to answer questions that might be asked by children of those ages. The primary task of sex education is a home responsibility, and churches can help parents feel more comfortable fulfilling that role.

To meet the needs of adults for a more comprehensive understanding of biblical and theological interpretations of sexuality, Thomas Tobey, Director of Pastoral Care and Counseling of the Mountain Brook Baptist Church, Birmingham, Alabama, conducted a five-week adult forum on "Sex and Love in the Bible." The content of the course was more inclusive than the title suggests since he dealt with Christian history, contemporary ethical attitudes, sex and love in Christian love, plus the

Old Testament and New Testament insights. Tobey prepared a detailed outline for the participants to use as a study guide.

Other churches approach sexual education by including it within the general framework of a family enrichment conference. When churches are just beginning a family ministry program, this method is less apt to create anxiety in people who feel threatened by sex education in the church. These methods can be adapted to churches of various sizes as the need for educational approaches to sexual education is developed.

---

**━Suggested Readings━**

Calderone, Mary S. and Johnson, Eric W. *The Family Book about Sexuality.* New York: Harper and Row, 1981.

Grant, W. Wilson. *From Parent to Child About Sex.* Grand Rapids: Zondervan, 1973.

Guernsey, Dennis. *Thoroughly Married.* Waco: Word Books, 1977.

Hollis, Jr., Harry. *Thank God for Sex.* Nashville: Broadman Press, 1975.

LaHaye, Tim and Beverly. *The Act of Marriage: The Beauty of Sexual Love.* Grand Rapids: Zondervan, 1976.

Penner, Clifford and Joyce. *The Gift of Sex: A Christian Guide to Sexual Fulfillment.*

---

## Life-style Choices: Singleness or Marriage

"In light of today's emphasis on personal freedom, what is the Christian attitude toward persons who choose to remain single instead of getting married?" This question from an attractive young adult choir member during a family enrichment conference in her church provoked a stimulating discussion concerning the relationship between biblical attitudes toward singleness and the contemporary world of single adults. How can this question be answered for Christian men and women today in a way that honestly reflects biblical teachings yet speaks to the needs of single adults in the churches?

### Biblical Backgrounds

First, we must accept the biblical world as one in which marriage, not singleness, was the assumed goal for young adults. There were widows, widowers, and divorcees in biblical times, but words are not found for spinsters (what a horrible word!) or bachelors in the original languages of the Bible. The virginal girl so prized by her parents and bridegroom was given in marriage by the time she was sixteen, so she had little chance to become an unmarried young adult. Her groom was usually only a few years older.

Marriage and family were necessary to reproduce the race, to sustain the economic system, and to give continuity to the family name. To remain unmarried was unusual in the cultural world of the Bible. Consequently, single adulthood was most often a result either of a broken marriage or some form of celibacy.

Whenever voluntary celibacy (the condition of remaining unmarried by choice) is mentioned in the Bible, it is in the context of a commitment to religious service which would be less effective if the person were married (Matt. 19:12; 1 Cor. 7:32-35). For example, in the life-styles of Jesus and Paul, voluntary celibacy was an integral part of their individual commitment to the will of God rather than a prescribed pattern of life for all Christians (Matt. 19:11; 1 Cor. 7:7).

Most forms of involuntary celibacy were due to birth defects or injury to the sexual organs which made sexual relations impossible. In such situations, marriage could not fulfill the biblical instructions for reproduction and therefore would not be a complete marriage. The Hebrews placed such supreme importance on the sexual potential of maleness that a male with injured sex organs could not even enter into the formal assembly of worship (Deut. 23:1).

For those who had been married, singleness could result from the death of a mate or divorce. For the woman, becoming single normally meant that some male had to be responsible for her. Consequently, remarriage after divorce or the death of a mate in Old Testament times was the expected practice (Deut. 24:1-4) unless she returned to her father's house to live under his care. In the New Testament, remarriage after divorce was frowned upon for Christians (1 Cor. 7:10-11), but remarriage of widows was encouraged (1 Tim. 5:14).

Since the cultural conditions of the biblical world influenced so greatly these biblical teachings, what changes in our contemporary world must be considered when we attempt to apply the thought of the Bible to our modern phenomena of single adulthood?

**Contemporary Realities**

*U.S. News and World Report* described the dramatic changes in the number and nature of single adults in the United States.[12] The following chart illustrates these changes.

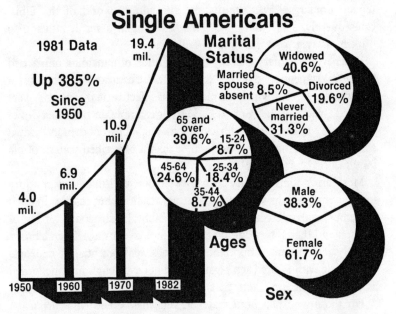

What factors have influenced such significant changes in life-style?

One very obvious change is the family structure itself. In the ancient world, the family consisted of the male head, his wife or wives, his sons with their wives and children, and his unmarried daughters. This type of extended family has changed in our world to the so-called nuclear family consisting of mother, father, and children who usually live apart from the older adult family members. Single young adults, therefore, are not as responsible to the family head as they were in the biblical world.

Also there is less emphasis on childbearing as a necessary goal for fulfillment in life. For example, the rate at which American women have children declined in 1972 to a rate below the level necessary to sustain zero population growth in the United States. When young adults decide that rearing children is not essential to total fulfillment, marriage is not as necessary. Of course, another factor is the growing number of single women who deliberately bear children without being married.

The lengthened time required for educating oneself to establish economic independence has influenced the growing population of single adults. In the biblical setting, young people in the extended family could marry and be supported by the family. This was the case with Jacob and his twelve sons. Today the young person often leaves home after high school to spend from four to six years getting established vocationally before marrying. The median age for first marriage has increased from 22.8 to 24.8 years for men and from 20.3 to 22.3 for women since 1960.

Attitudes have also changed concerning the necessity of marriage at all. University of Michigan researchers Arland Thorton and Deborah Freedman conducted a study of American attitudes toward singleness based upon an 18-year intergenerational study of 916 families in the Detroit area supplemented by several other national studies.[13] Even though 90 percent of the 18-year-olds questioned believed that they would marry, only 25 percent of those young men and women said it would bother them a great deal to remain single. Another 25 percent said it would bother them only a little.

One of the interesting findings was that mothers of those 18-year-olds, mothers who had first been interviewed in 1962, were more accepting of singleness as a life-style for their children than would have been expected. Over 40 percent of the mothers said it would not bother them if a son or daughter did not marry, and only 10 percent affirmed that it would bother them a great deal.

Perhaps one of the most significant changes is the freedom of women today to support themselves apart from their family of origin without depending on marriage for economic security. The United States Department of Labor reported in 1982 that women made up 53 percent of the nation's total work force. This factor has also influenced the possibility of divorce when a woman finds marriage unsatisfactory.

Thus we must be willing to interpret the Bible against the backdrop of our contemporary culture rather than simply trying to ignore the influence of the ancient culture on biblical thought. Christian choices today are not dependent on the economic and familiar setting of the Old Testament world.

## Choosing as a Christian

The value of individual personhood as implied in Galatians 3:28 is a major contribution to our understanding of human life. An individual can find wholesome fulfillment in life as a single person if one's self-concept is accepting and healthy. As was discussed earlier in this chapter, to know that one has total acceptance with God by faith and that there is equality of personhood with all others in the gospel is affirming and self-assuring. This is a key to happy Christian life as a single adult, whether singleness is the result of choice, divorce, or widowhood.

Donna L. Peterson, a French teacher from Winnetka, Illinois, is a never-married Christian single teaching in a large public high school with a faculty of over two hundred. Many of the faculty **are single**, most by their own choice. She decided to do her own mini-survey of her Christian friends at church and of her non-Christian friends on the faculty concerning their sense of self-worth as singles.

Among the school teachers, she found generally a positive self-image which she attributed to the large number of them, to the fact that no one felt discriminated against because of marital status, and to their economic resources for enjoying the "good life." By contrast, it was from her Christian friends that she found negative reactions to the word *single*.

Reflecting on her mini-survey, Miss Peterson declared, "It is paradoxical that Christians, who believe that they are made in the image of God and that Jesus Christ loved them so much that He died to redeem them, have a poor self-image. Instead of developing their sense of self-worth as children of God, they feel inferior because they have not married." Of course, she went on to point out, there were single Christians responding to her question who did have a very positive self-image.[14]

Jesus' emphasis on the right to choose celibacy as a definite life-style must be reaffirmed. Because of the basic family-centeredness of the Bible and our family ministry programs, it is possible for single adults to be looked upon as oddballs who are failing to fulfill God's basic plan for human life. Wholeness as persons must never be identified with marriage in the same way that completeness in intimacy is identified with the one-flesh union.

Paul certainly supported the right to singleness in his affirmation that each person received his or her own gift from God with regard to being able to live the single life creatively (1 Cor. 7:7). The gift, or charisma, from God is the empowerment to live singly without being overwhelmed by sexual tension. Because of the challenge of ministry in a world to which Christ would soon return (1 Cor. 7:29), Paul wished that everyone could remain content in the condition in which the call to Christ was first received—married, single, slave, free, whatever. He particularly encouraged singles who had the gift of continence to remain unmarried, but, at the same time, he gave full approval to marriage if it were desired. *The Living Bible* paraphrases the charisma of grace as "the gift of being able to stay happily unmarried" (1 Cor. 7:7).

Based on this word of Paul, Donna Peterson describes her own philosophy of singleness: "Rather than seeing singleness as a terrible fate, one should accept it as a grace-gift from God, an opportunity to lead a productive life, enjoying all of its benefits." This gift of grace comes to the never-married, but it is also potentially available to the divorced and widowed.

The Christian single therefore faces these choices: (1) not to marry, (2) to marry, (3) to remarry after death or divorce of a mate. Churches can help provide resources for decision to singles in each category.

## Programs for Singles

How can churches help meet the needs of single adults? Perhaps a start can be made by determining what those needs really are. Never-married as well as divorced and widowed singles may need supportive counseling about their life goals and opportunities for meeting other singles. Village United Presbyterian Church in Prairie Village, Kansas, found this to be true in its program for singles. About twenty years ago several persons going through divorce reached out to each other and began support groups for divorced people whether church members or not. Today about two thousand single persons a month participate in singles activities sponsored by the church.

Cheryl Hammock Turner, full-time director of singles programming and counseling, indicates that a church-sponsored work with singles can provide a caring, loving atmosphere in which "one can seek friendship, personal growth, living enrichment, fun times and . . . spiritual fulfillment." Since she had remained single until 27 years of age, married and then divorced, Ms. Turner is well aware of the needs that singles bring into church-sponsored activities. She maintains that in the larger metropolitan areas, such as greater Kansas City, "Every church in this community could open up for singles programs and there still wouldn't be enough to meet the needs of the community."

At the Wieuca Road Baptist Church, Atlanta, Georgia, only seven people were enrolled in the church's single adult Sunday School department in 1970. Now the membership has increased to almost one thousand with seven different categories of age groups for them. According to Betty Yates, director of the single adult division, singles have been joining the Sunday School in large numbers during the last three to six years. The church program includes Bible studies each Tuesday and Wednesday plus monthly seminars, social events, and sporting activities for singles. "The emphasis here is not strictly on developing relationships or dating," declared Mrs. Yates. "We stress that you are a whole person as a single." However, in most church situations, creating a setting within which relationships will develop is part of the ministry opportunity.

Divorced and widowed men and women often find that it is very difficult to reenter the dating life in seeking companionship and, therefore, may withdraw into their shells rather than venture out into society. Parents without partners face the added difficulty of caring for children after work when they are also hungry for adult companionship and affection.

The church's role, therefore, includes providing opportunities for singles to find fulfillment through ministry to others, to meet other singles socially, to have child-care assistance so they can get out of the home on occasion, and perhaps to assist them in practical ways such as home maintenance and legal protection.

Single adults need acceptance, fellowship, and love. Christ's church is the place where all of these should be found. But singles also need help in preparing for the marriages that most of them will one day consummate. Whether it is a first marriage or a return to marriage from divorce or widowhood, churches can contribute to the development of strong marriages through their family ministry programs. This is the challenge of the next chapter.

---

**Suggested Readings**

Anders, Sarah Frances. *Woman Alone: Confident and Creative.* Nashville: Broadman Press, 1976.

Brown, Raymond Kay. *Reach Out to Singles: A Challenge to Ministry.* Philadelphia: Westminster Press, 1979.

Collins, Gary. *It's O. K. to Be Single.* Waco: Word Books, 1976.

Dow, Robert Arthur. *Ministry With Single Adults.* Valley Forge: Judson Press, 1977.

Hugen, Walter D. *The Church's Ministry to the Older Unmarried.* Grand Rapids: Eerdmans, 1960.

Smith, Ann Alexander. *How to Start a Single Adult Ministry.* Nashville: Material Services.

Wood, Britton. *Single Adults Want to Be the Church, Too.* Nashville: Broadman Press, 1977.

# 5
# Developing Strong Marriages

I am firmly in agreement with the person who remarked, "Most marriages are not made in heaven; they come in kits, and you have to put them together yourself!" A good marriage does not happen by accident—it is created by persons who make a conscious commitment to develop a relationship in which mutual need-making is primary as each partner seeks to understand and relate to the basic needs of the other. An educational responsibility of the church is to help couples enter marriage more knowledgeably and experience marriage more understandably. This chapter will explore some ways that churches are attempting to fulfill these objectives.

## Premarital Guidance

In 1978, *The Baptist Program* carried an article by Jimmy Smith, then minister of youth of the Casa View Baptist Church in Mesquite, Texas, describing the policy of the church requiring mandatory premarital counseling for couples to be married by any of the ministers of the church or in the church building.[1] He pointed out that the original motivation for such a program came from a twofold tension felt by the staff: (1) their concern over the high divorce rate in America, and (2) the need to clarify the roles of minister and church in their roles of conducting marriages.

The program was set up using lay counselors selected and trained by the pastor. Six one-hour sessions were established and the charge per couple at that time was twenty dollars to cover the cost of materials. Brochures were printed and mailed to the entire membership describing the plan, and it was enthusiastically adopted by the church.

By 1982 the program had continued to be a vital part of the church's family ministry program. Mrs. Michele Cosby, premarriage coordinator, indicated that there were thirteen trained counselors available to meet with couples desiring marriage in the church. A committee had been formed to oversee the program to relieve the pastor of that responsibility. In the course of the counseling, the Taylor-Johnson Temperament Analysis and the Marriage Expectation Inventory are used to assist the couples to understand each other as persons and in clarifying their individual anticipations for marriage. The six one-hour sessions have been retained as the basic model although modifications are made in this schedule when necessary.

The Casa View Baptist Church has taken seriously its responsibility to help couples marry with greater understanding of marriage and can serve as a good model for other churches. But perhaps you have said or heard said, "Premarital guidance is a waste of time. They are so wrapped up in love that they don't hear anything you tell them!" Maybe the fault is in the approach rather than in the couple. Let us examine some of the implications of research for effective premarital guidance.

## Nature of Premarital Guidance

I prefer the term *guidance* rather than *counseling* for the educational work that is done prior to a wedding since the minister takes a much greater initiative in programming it than he generally does in the counseling role. This guidance centers around the interpersonal relationships of the man and woman about to be married and seeks to help them understand each other more completely as well as to evaluate their own readiness for marriage. It includes didactic material but functions best when it is experiential for the couple.

One of the most helpful studies of the effectiveness of premarital guidance was conducted by Claude A. Guldner when he was serving as a clinical pastoral education (CPE) supervisor in Denver, Colorado. With CPE interns as group facilitators, couples who had experienced some form of premarital guidance were interviewed about its impact on their marriages. Strikingly the majority of the couples remembered very little of their sessions with the minister.

To test various approaches to premarital guidance, Guldner and his associates placed couples who were planning to be married in eight different groups with formats ranging from primarily didactic to interactional group activity under a facilitator. In the evaluations at the close of the session and a follow-up one year later, the most effective learning experiences were shared by those who had been in a group designed to cover seven sessions with each session having specific goals and purposes. At each session, these goals and purposes were briefly presented and then the couples engaged in couple or small group exercises designed to stimulate personal sharing on those issues.[2]

The lesson is clear. If clergy or laypersons see premarital guidance as primarily a teaching tool to tell people about marriage, the couple will probably remember little about it. If it is seen as an opportunity for helping couples talk to each other in a directed fashion about their own needs, dreams, and feelings, then premarital guidance can be a worthwhile enterprise.

## Purposes of Premarital Guidance

Even though I have already intimated some of the purposes, let me highlight them in this section. (1) One purpose is to guide the couple in a general preparation for marriage through the readings, homework assignments, and input from the person or persons providing the guidance. This includes such goals as gaining insight into their personal maturity for marriage, exploring their role understandings, developing insight into communication skills, and introducing conflict resolution models. (2) A second purpose is to deal with the planning of the wedding itself which includes developing the form of wedding ceremony that is desired by the couple and approved by the church. (3) A third purpose is to deal with specific problems of which the couple may be aware in preparing for their lives together. These problem areas may be spiritual, physical, economic, psychological, or related to family attitudes toward their wedding. This particular purpose may surface quite frequently when the persons considering marriage are divorced or widowed and have to deal with prior marital experiences. For some senior adults, there may be problems with their grown children that need to be talked through. These problems may bring the couple for premarital counseling, or the problems may arise during the scheduled interviews.

(4) A fourth purpose or goal of premarital care is to lay a groundwork for future counseling. By establishing a good rapport with the couple, the pastor or church representatives can encourage counseling help in the future if problems develop which threaten the marriage. When a couple has been helped before their marriage by the minister, they have a greater tendency to trust counseling through the church as a means to conflict resolution. In fact, this can be encouraged in the premarital program.

## Procedures in Premarital Guidance

There are many patterns of premarital work that can fulfill these stated purposes. The pastor's own temperament, his training, and his attitude toward being involved with couples will influence the method chosen. At this point I would simply reaffirm what Guldner discovered— involving the couple in their own interaction is imperative to whatever procedure is chosen.

1. *Use the wedding ceremony as a guide.* Ministers may enhance the meaning of marriage and the seriousness of the vows by centering their premarital interviews around the wedding ceremony itself. Wayne Oates and Wade Rowatt point out the values of such an approach in their premarital guidebook *Before You Marry Them.*

2. *Use a book as a guide.* For many years ministers have used *Harmony in Marriage* by Leland Foster Wood as a gift book for couples. It can also serve as a guide to the premarital sessions. Having the couple read assigned chapters prior to each interview provides a basis for shared discussion of their feelings and responses to the written material.

My own *Christian Marriage: Growing in Oneness* has also been used by ministers for that purpose. Other books used by ministers are David R.

Mace's *Getting Ready for Marriage*, Cliff Allbritton's *How to Get Married and Stay that Way*, Jerry and Karen Hayner's *Marriage Can Be Meaningful*, and *Marriage Readiness* by Bobbye and Britton Wood.

3. *Use a workbook approach.* Several resources are available that provide a manual for the facilitator and a workbook for the couple. The counselor follows the plan set forth in the manual which is keyed to the homework assignments for the couple. *Two as One*, a Christian marriage preparation program designed by Jesuit priest George E. Von Kaenel and family life specialist Martin G. Olsen, can be used with non-Catholic couples as well as with Catholics. It requires three sessions of about two and a half hours, preferably completed in one week. Effective use of the materials can also be done in a weekend engaged couples retreat.

James R. Hine's *Grounds for Marriage* includes a workbook which requires the couple to fill out several questionnaires and suggests additional reading for each area of discussion.

4. *Prepare one's own guide.* In order to give consideration to the topics or relationships which are most significant to the individual minister or committee of the church, the preparation of a guide suitable for such purposes can be developed and reproduced for the couples. While serving as pastor in Texas, I had occasion to marry six couples within a two-month period who had been friends for many years as they grew up in the church. I conducted a six-week discussion time with the couples as a group using my own mimeographed outline to guide our conversations. This guide has been revised from time to time and still serves its purpose of giving direction to premarital sessions.

## Number of Interviews

The minister will soon recognize that flexibility with regard to a specified number of interviews will be essential as schedules of the couple and the counselor must be taken into account. In some cases, particularly involving couples who are not members of the church, there may be only one conference with a couple before the wedding. In most cases, however, the desired range seems to be from three to six interviews with at least one follow-up visit at some time after the marriage has begun. More will be said about this followup visit later.

## Subjects to Be Considered

The procedure chosen by the minister or church will obviously affect the subject matter for the sessions, but it is important to encourage the couple to discuss issues that can cause trouble in their marriage. Among these factors are: anger patterns, how do they deal with anger now and how their parents handle it; feelings about children, including desire for and discipline of children; relationship to their in-laws, how they have dealt with attachment to the primary family unit; money and how they will handle it, including their attitudes toward the wife working out of the home; vocational goals, including any schooling necessary to achieve those goals.

Four other items of considerable importance are their attitudes toward maintaining friendships formed during single years; their felt needs for tenderness, closeness, and appreciation from each other; their value systems including religious fulfillment; and their communication patterns.

Claude Guldner in cooperation with Ed Bader, a Toronto psychologist, developed a process model using groups of couples who meet for seven sessions. The first session is for establishing rapport and providing testing materials to be completed by the participants. They use the Taylor-Johnson Temperament Analysis along with other inventories. Successive sessions deal with attitudes toward love and marriage, self-systems having origins in their primary families, daily activities of married life, emotional or feeling dimensions of their relationship, affectional and sexual aspects of their marriage, and conclude with spiritual valuing and goals for their marriage. This is a very comprehensive look at the dynamics of marital relationships, and its very breadth may frighten some ministers from attempting such a program. It is always possible for a minister to deal with many of these issues without having the counselor training of Guldner and his associates, however, so consider how you may be able to integrate these areas of concern into your own program.

## Methods of Premarital Guidance

The majority of ministers will probably plan their own program and meet with individual couples as weddings are scheduled in the church. If so, the minister can demonstrate his own commitment to premarital guidance by requiring or encouraging couples to meet with him for guidance early enough before the wedding to deal with these significant concerns. The closer the couple gets to the wedding, the less time and energy will they have to examine the marriage!

Some churches will use the approach of Casa View Baptist Church in Texas with lay counselors chosen and trained to do the premarital guidance. The minister(s) of the church may participate in some phases of that program, but it is essentially a lay training activity.

In other situations where weddings occur frequently throughout the year, churches may schedule regular group sessions for all couples planning to be married during a particular time frame. Leadership of these groups may be by ministers or by laypersons, but emphasis must be placed on regular attendance for group solidarity to develop.

The engaged couples retreat has also developed as an off-shoot of the marriage enrichment retreat program. Couples who are already planning their weddings or who are seriously committed to marriage, even though no date has been set, are invited to a weekend experience designed to deal with the issues already mentioned. Getting away from the regular routines has a valuable contribution to make to engaged couples as well as to married persons.

## Post-Wedding Checkup

One of the interesting by-products of Guldner's research was the value of a follow-up session with couples at some time after the wedding. He found that scheduling such visits one month after the wedding was ineffective because problem areas had not yet begun to surface. It is hard to see storm clouds when you have stars in your eyes! Couples married three months were becoming aware of problems but were not comfortable facing them. Couples married six months or more, however, were ready to deal openly and therapeutically with issues that had surfaced in the marriage.

Many ministers are now requesting couples to meet with them in this type of post-wedding checkup. Some ministers take note of the date and send a reminder to the couple to ensure that they will return for the interview. Other ministers leave the return interview to the discretion of the couple but encourage it. Certainly such a visit at the initiation of the minister does have validity as a means of resolving beginning problems. Since the minister has requested them to come, the couple does not need to feel that they are having problems serious enough to call for counseling.

The nature of the post-wedding interview is usually to reflect on the issues discussed in the premarital sessions with a view toward helping the couple talk through any issues that have become significant, as well as to share their fulfillment in the marriage.

---

**Resources for Premarital Guidance**

1. *Books on premarital guidance.*

   Gangsei, Lyle B. *Manual for Group Premarital Counseling*. New York: Association, 1971.

   Hulme, William E. *The Pastoral Care of Families: Its Theology and Practice*. New York: Abingdon, 1962.

   Morris, J. Kenneth. *Premarital Counseling: A Manual for Ministers*. Englewood Cliffs, NJ: Prentice-Hall, 1960.

   Oates, Wayne E. and Rowatt, Wade. *Before You Marry Them*. Nashville: Broadman Press, 1975.

2. *Inventories, Tests.*

   Marriage Expectation Inventory for Engaged Couples, Marital Communications Inventory, Sex Knowledge Inventory: Family Life Publications, Inc.

---

### Marriage Enrichment Programs

Marriage and family enrichment is the new kid on the block for church programming with the first reported marriage enrichment program having been conducted by David R. Mace in 1961. Since that time, enrichment programs have become the fastest growing segment of preventive ministry to families among church groups, as well as professional therapists. Its basic philosophy is founded on the growth potential emphasis of contemporary psychology and on the belief that every family can be helped to achieve greater fulfillment in interpersonal living by guidance in understanding its potential and removing whatever blocks there may be to growing toward that potential. Enrichment programs are essentially designed for healthy marriages and families, not for troubled persons who may need therapy rather than enrichment.

*Marriage* enrichment programs are for couples who wish to improve their generally satisfactory marriages whereas *family* enrichment programs are directed toward parents and children together in their desire to enhance the interpersonal relationships of the family members. In this section, attention will be given to marriage enrichment, and family enrichment will be considered in chapter 6.

What are some means that churches are using or can use to fulfill the goals of marriage enrichment?

## Group Studies on Christian Marriage

One popular means of marital education is group study of marital relationships utilizing resources available through denominational publishing houses or from independent specialists in the marriage field. These study groups may meet Sunday morning or evening, during the week for a regularly scheduled period of time, or in a concentrated experience for a whole day or weekend.

*The Intimate Marriage* by Howard and Charlotte Clinebell is an excellent resource book for such a study. It focuses on the development of a more open marriage in the communication of feelings and needs along with a consideration of the various functional adjustments necessary to a growing marriage. Each chapter includes assigned exercises for couples to work on for the enrichment of their own marriage after having participated in the group discussion period.

Carolyn and Bill Self wrote *A Survival Kit for Marriage* to be used in a Sunday School department for newlyweds and newly reweds. Since that time it has been used well in seminars and group study sessions outside of the Sunday School organization. It is divided into sections dealing with the meaning of marriage, the need for self and other understanding, communication, religion, growing through the life cycle, and celebrating the marriage. Each chapter closes with a work space for each individual to answer questions that will then be used in group discussion. The questions are for personal reflection and the sharing of individual feelings and hopes for marital fulfillment.

Southern Baptists have developed training modules for group use in the churches. Each module contains material for the leader and for the group in dealing with the issue under consideration. Modules in the family field have been the most popular of the many being produced, and more are available for marriage and family then for any other subject.

As a resource for the third year of their four-year emphasis on strengthening families (1982-1985), two modules were developed for 1984 when the churches study *Christian Marriage: Growing in Oneness.* One module, *Before You Marry,* is for couples planning marriage, and the other, *Your Marriage: Growing in Oneness,* is for married couples. Both of these are recommended for group study at the church or in homes of members.

In addition to general books discussing the whole range of marital interactions, groups are also involved in studying selected areas of marriage such as conflict resolution, financial planning, sexual relationships, and communication.

Pleasant Valley Baptist Church, near Kansas City, Missouri, annually includes marriage and family studies in its School of Disciples meeting on Sunday evening at the church. During a recent quarter, members were offered the options of participating in seminars dealing with "Straight Talk to Men and their Wives" using the book by James Dobson, "Husbands and Wives: Studying the Bible Together" using the book of that title published by the Navigators, "Advanced Christian Interpersonal Communication," and "Men and Mid-life Crisis."

In planning group studies of marriage, ministers and other leaders will need to carefully review the materials under consideration in order to understand the perspective of the authors. For example, a group studying my own *Equality and Submission in Marriage* will be exposed to a very different theological approach to marital relationships than if they study *How to Be Happy Though Married* by Tim LaHaye. This review of materials is not intended as a censuring device but in order to help the group deal openly with the material presented. Exposure to insights different from one's own can contribute to marital growth when this is done in an attitude of shared learning.

Group studies in marriage have the advantage of being open to persons who are not married or whose mates will not attend the sessions, whereas marriage enrichment activities often are planned specifically for couples to attend together. Thus this form of marital education is very popular in the churches. Let us remember the insight of David Mace, however, that the implementation of such education in some form of behavioral change is dependent on encouraging couples to do the prescribed exercises between sessions.

## Marriage Enrichment Retreats and Seminars

1. *Retreats.* Retreats are often scheduled for a weekend beginning on Friday evening and continuing through Saturday evening or Sunday morning. Usually best results depend on the retreat being in a location which will permit the couples to have a bedroom to themselves as well as providing a large conference space for the entire group and smaller rooms or locations for small group activities. Even though retreats can be held in church facilities with the couples returning home for the night, this is less than ideal. One aspect of the learning process depends on the couple being free of normal home responsibilities in order to concentrate on their marriage. Returning home to the children and emotional surroundings of the marriage in the middle of the retreat makes this more difficult.

A growing trend in marriage enrichment retreats is for the leadership to be done by couples trained through experience and education to be facilitators. The Association of Couples for Marriage Enrichment

(ACME) founded by David and Vera Mace is one of the organizations that trains and certifies retreat leaders around the country. Even among professional family life specialists, the husband and wife often conduct the retreats as a team rather than as individuals. In this way, the leader couple becomes a model in interaction for the persons attending the retreat.

The range of planned experiences in retreats is so broad that it is difficult to encompass them all in this brief chapter. Marriage Encounter, which began as a Roman Catholic approach in 1967, places the enrichment process in dialogue, written and verbal, between the married partners with little or no group support or interaction. Educational input comes through lectures by the minister or couple facilitators, and the remainder of the time is devoted to personal interaction of the couple with one another. On the other hand, retreats which emphasize enrichment rather than encounter include input sessions by the leader(s), personal interaction by the couple, and group experiences in which the couples share with other group members some of the material they have discussed as couples. Group support in this model becomes an important part of the learning process.

One of the exercises which I have found helpful involves having one couple sit in "sharing chairs" while the four or five other couples in their particular group sit around them. Each person in the group will have privately written answers to such statements as "These are the ways that you show me that you love me." The husband is asked to share with his wife the things which he has written, and then she shares with him her list. After each couple has had an opportunity to be in the sharing chairs, the group discusses with each other their feelings about what they have heard and shared.

At the conclusion of such an exercise, I asked the participants, "Did you feel uncomfortable sharing these personal things in the group?" Almost universally the answer was, "No, at least not after we had gotten started doing it. It seemed like we were really just talking to each other as a couple rather than in front of a group." Upon being asked if they felt like spectators while others were in the sharing chairs, the normal response is that they felt like participants in the experience rather than on-lookers.

Why would couples be asked to express their feelings before such a group anyway? One purpose is to enable them to hear how other men and women experience the meaning of love in their marriages. There is a valuable contribution to one's own marriage in being able to say to another group member, "Hey, I liked the way you said that. I have thought about that before but never really knew how to tell my wife what I felt!" Marriage enrichment models which utilize group process discover it to have effective power for the change process.

For example, one couple attending a retreat was not ready to enter into the exercise when the retreat began on Friday evening. They did not do the written assignments and sat silently when others were sharing their experiences. The group still welcomed them and treated them warmly. During Saturday morning, the couple began to do a little more of the written work; by Saturday afternoon, they were entering into the group discussions. When the retreat was concluding, the wife said, "Thank you for giving us the freedom to be listeners only and still be accepted. We have been struggling with some pretty heavy conflict lately and did not feel comfortable doing the assignments. Now, with your help, we feel better prepared to really work on building our marriage."

This leads us to emphasize three covenantal relationships that are significant to the success of retreats. One, participation in the assigned work is voluntary, especially with reference to group sharing. Often one of the partners coming may be what is humorously called "the draggee," the person who really did not want to come but did at the mate's insistence. Putting pressure on that person for participation may be more detrimental than helpful. Two, there must be a covenant of confidentiality. During the process of the retreat, some couples will be sharing very personal realities about their own lives or marriages as they seek to clarify the meaning of their relationship. Trusting the other retreat participants to respect those revelations as privileged information helps the couples to be honest with themselves and with each other. Any participant is free after the retreat to tell other people things which he or she may have said but is not free to share what others said without their permission to do so.

Third is the covenant to remain for the entire retreat. The progression of growth desired in the retreat depends on a couple sharing the full experience with each other. This is one of the fundamental differences between an informational session and an experiential session. Information can be shared without couple cooperation, but marriage enrichment dealing with behaviors is most effective when they work on the assignments together over the full weekend.

Southern Baptists, through the Family Ministry Program of the Baptist Sunday School Board, have developed a Baptist Marriage Enrichment System which includes a Marriage Enrichment Sampler, a Basic Marriage Enrichment Retreat, a Marriage Enrichment Leadership Training Workshop, and are working on plans for an advanced retreat. The sampler is approximately twenty-four hours in length whereas the basic is forty-one hours. Attendance at a Basic retreat is required prior to attending the leadership workshop for couples who desire to be certified by the program as qualified leader couples.

The Association of Couples for Marriage Enrichment has local chapters throughout the country which conduct retreats and train leaders. ACME utilizes the dialogue method initiated by David and Vera Mace as the format for their retreats. Participants identify their particular areas of concern at the beginning of the retreat and the leader couple will demonstrate how they might dialogue together on one of those issues. The attending couples are then taught principles of communication and dialogue by which they can deal with such concerns as sexual fulfillment, anger resolution, and emotional need fulfillment. ACME groups are normally sponsored by church organizations in the community.

These two retreat styles have been described in some detail because they are church centered and can be led by persons from the church who qualify as leader couples through the training programs mentioned. In many cases, ministers and their wives are becoming qualified leaders in order to lead retreats for their own members or for other churches.

The majority of people who participate in a retreat usually have a good experience and become ambassadors for marriage enrichment to their friends. It is important, however, to realize that everyone may not have such a positive response. This is due at times to the nature of the retreat and at times to unrealizable expectations brought by the participants. Leaders may insist that their own program must be followed to the letter if the retreat is to be effective, and this in itself can create problem situations for participants who struggle to fulfill those specific instructions.

For example, one expectation of Marriage Encounter is that couples will continue the writing and dialoging of feelings each week after the retreat. Therapists have had counselees whose basic marital conflict was related to mixed feelings about doing this assignment. When one partner is convinced that this weekly program must be completed and the mate does not consider it necessary, conflict does occur.

Another possible problem in the marriage enrichment retreat is offering simplistic answers to complex issues in human relationships. When these answers do not meet the needs of couples in their daily interaction, they may reject the retreat as unrealistic to life. In doing so, they also may turn away from solid psychological or religious training in other aspects of the marriage enrichment program.

Certainly the retreat leaders will offer guidelines for developing more fulfilling marriages, but flexibility remains an essential element in describing what marriages can be. Imposing one's own particular model on all couples will create frustration for some and resentment by others, as well as acceptance by a large group of the participants.

In spite of these potential problem areas, marriage enrichment retreats are one of the most powerful preventive tools available to the churches for strengthening Christian marriage and avoiding marital dry rot. My research indicates that many church members would like to participate in a retreat program. Of the married respondents to the survey, 11.7 percent did not answer the question, 44.6 percent said yes, they would like to attend a marriage enrichment retreat, and 43.7 percent said no. It is interesting to note that 49.8 percent of the pastors would like to be in a retreat, but only 39.2 percent of the remarried persons said yes. Of the intact families, 42.2 percent responded affirmatively.

Some negative votes may have been cast because of wrong impressions about marriage enrichment retreats, but the strong desire for participation is an encouragement for churches to plan for them.

2. *Seminars.* The primary distinction between the retreat and the seminar as a marriage enrichment activity is the length of time required rather than the subject matter considered. Seminars for marital enrichment may require the same commitment to attendance by the couple as the retreat, but the sessions are spread over several weeks rather than several days. This change poses some difficulty for using outside leadership but it is an effective style of enrichment.

On one occasion I had opportunity to lead a marriage enrichment seminar for military personnel at Fort Leavenworth, Kansas. The three-hour Sunday afternoon session continued for five weeks with assigned homework to be completed during the week between sessions. Interest remained high, and the attendance record was excellent even though some of the personnel had to meet assigned work responsibilities on one or two of the Sundays.

Several psychologists in Texas conducted an experiment to test the difference in marital growth experienced by couples attending a weekend retreat in comparison with other couples attending a five-week program. They used several testing instruments to measure change in order to avoid relying primarily on subjective comments. The testing instruments were used prior to participation in each program, and then the participants joined in a follow-up evaluation session twelve weeks after the end of the retreat and the seminar when the same tests were used again.

Statistical change was limited for a number of the areas tested, but the general trend of the results showed more change for couples who had participated in the five-week group than in the weekend group. Wives regularly showed more change than men, although men did register change in areas reflecting greater concensus with wives in their marriages.[3] Even though the particular model used might condition the ability to apply their findings to all programs, their results do suggest that some couples can have significant marital growth experiences while meeting for two-hour weekly sessions over a period of several weeks.

Second Baptist Church, Lubbock, Texas, uses this approach in planning a number of seminars related to marriage and family. The groups meet two hours weekly for ten weeks at a time and place selected by the participants. The marriage enrichment group used the Clinebells' book, *The Intimate Marriage*, with the stated purpose of helping couples learn skills of relating in depth. Each group was limited to five to six couples to facilitate personal interaction within the group.

## Marital Growth Groups

Another approach to marriage enrichment is the marital growth group which covenants to meet over an extended period of time rather than for a five- to ten-week stated study program. Growth groups often utilize written or audiovisual resources as aids to interaction but a primary focus is on personal sharing and encouragement.[4]

Roy and Kay Woodruff began a marital growth group while living in Kansas City in the mid-1970s. After meeting with the group for a couple of years, Dr. Woodruff became the director of Peninsular Counseling Center in Hampton, Virginia. When the Woodruffs came to our home recently for a visit, they were later to meet with that same growth group which had continued to meet regularly for over five years. This illustrates how some groups may continue to respond to the needs of couples for mutual support over a long period of time.

## Personal Study

Having considered various ways that churches use group activities for marriage enrichment, it is also important to recognize that churches may encourage individual couples to enrich their own marriages by studying and reflecting on some of the books or audiocassettes designed for this purpose. *How to Have a Happy Marriage* by the Maces is written as a step-by-step guide to an enriched relationship in language that is easy for any couple to understand and follow. *The Intimate Marriage* and *A*

*Survival Kit for Marriage* are each usable by individuals. Through its media resources, churches can encourage couples to use these materials by publicizing them in the newsletters sent to members.

Personal study lacks some of the learning experiences that group participation provides, but it can be an excellent means for personal reflection on one's marriage and its potential for growth.

These, then, are some ways that churches can strengthen existing marriages that are reasonably satisfactory but need stimulus to grow. This is an educational opportunity that challenges church planning. It is also true, however, that ministry to troubled marriages is an inescapable responsibility and a significant opportunity for the church and its people. We turn now to look at remedial ministry to marriages.

---

**Suggested Reading**

Clinebell, Howard and Charlotte. *The Intimate Marriage*. New York: Harper and Row, 1970.

Dale, Robert D. and Carrie K. *Making Good Marriages Better: A Guidebook for Marriage Enrichment*. Nashville: Broadman Press, 1978.

Hendrix, John, ed. *On Becoming a Group*. Nashville: Broadman Press, n.d.

Howell, John C. *Christian Marriage: Growing in Oneness*. Nashville: Convention Press, 1983.

Kilgore, James. *Try Marriage Before Divorce*. Waco: Word, 1978.

Mace, David and Vera. *Marriage Enrichment in the Church*. Nashville: Broadman Press, 1976.

_____. *How To Have A Happy Marriage*. Nashville: Abingdon, 1977.

Otto, Herbert A., ed. *Marriage and Family Enrichment: New Perspectives and Programs*. Nashville: Abingdon, 1976.

Self, Carolyn S. and William L. *A Survival Kit for Marriage*. Nashville: Broadman Press, 1981.

---

## Ministry to Troubled Marriages

The telephone rang during supper. The pastor who called was asking for help in responding to the hurting marriage of a couple in his church. The couple had attended two marriage enrichment retreats sponsored by the church and had shared one evening session at the church dealing with marital relationships. In spite of these enrichment experiences, they were now seriously considering divorce, evidently due in part to some fundamental differences in personality style. Both were active in the church, but their marriage was in trouble.

Cries for help when marriages are hurting come regularly to persons in ministry. There is no way that a caring church will escape the emotional impact of giving itself freely to persons struggling with a marriage that fails to fulfill the expectations or needs of the marriage partners. Churches can respond to these cries for help in at least three significant ways: marriage counseling by the pastor, lay support systems, and remedial marriage retreats.

## Pastoral Marriage Counseling

Wayne Oates confronted the minister with inescapable logic when he wrote, "The pastor, regardless of his training, does not enjoy the privilege of electing whether or not he will counsel with his people. They inevitably bring their problems to him for his best guidance and wisest care. He cannot avoid this if he stays in the pastoral ministry."[5] As indicated in chapter 3, his preaching style will be a factor in encouraging people to know that a listening ear is available when trouble becomes a reality for them. Marriage counseling is one phase of that counseling ministry.

1. *Definition*. When dealing with troubled marriages, pastoral counselors need to remember that the relationship is as much the client as the two persons sitting in his study. Marriage counseling, therefore, is the process by which the counselor assists two persons to develop their abilities for resolving the difficulties inherent in their interpersonal relationship to a degree acceptable to both of the partners. Each of the partners will have certain problems with the relationship and the counselor's task or goal is to see if they can find a workable solution to marital stress, to help them develop coping responses if change cannot occur, or to assist them to face realistically the issues involved in separation if they decide not to remain married.

2. *Approaches.* Marital counseling will follow one or more of four possible approaches to the counseling task. Determining which one to use may be influenced by the counselor's training or by the nature of the presented problem from one or more of the marital partners.

(1) Individual counseling with one member of the marriage. Ministers regularly become engaged in dealing with marriages in trouble because one mate requests an appointment to talk about their relationship. Most often the wife will be the first to seek help when trouble is developing, and she may be convinced that her husband will not join her in counseling. When approached in this way, the minister may elect to counsel with that partner and not require or insist that the mate also share the counseling relationship.

Even though some therapists will not do individual counseling for a troubled marriage, it is possible for the minister to help one person evaluate his or her behavior with a view to constructive change so that the relationship can be improved. In this approach, the minister's role is not to give sympathy or to overidentify with the one partner but to help that person assess the system of interaction going on in the marriage. Attention is focused on the behavior of the mate in counseling rather than the one not coming. Obviously, this is not usually what the person seeking help expects!

"I didn't come here to talk about me, I came here to talk about him," exclaimed the wife to her pastor when he kept probing her about her behavior in the marriage. However, because marriages are systems of interpersonal interaction, changing one component of the system can reorder the whole nature of the relationship. When this wife learned some tools for relating better to her husband's moods, without simply becoming angry, the marriage became more rewarding, and the husband ultimately was willing to come for counseling with his wife.

A biblical example of the influence of one person in a marriage can be seen in Peter's instructions to wives of non-Christian mates. He encouraged them to give voluntary yieldedness in love to their husbands in testimony of their own faith in Christ. Through their personal behavior, some of the husbands, "though they do not obey the word, may be won without a word by the behavior of their wives, when they see your reverent and chaste behavior" (1 Pet. 3:1-2). This is not an appeal for wives to submit without protest to any kind of treatment husbands may give them, but it is counsel for marital happiness when husbands and wives disagree on a basic issue such as shared Christian faith.

(2) Concurrent counseling with both partners. In this approach, the minister does counsel with both persons in the marriage but sees them separately. Concurrent counseling may be utilized because of the unwillingness of the couple to come together or because the minister believes that separate sessions are necessary to get to the heart of the issue.

One of the problems with concurrent counseling is that the minister hears things from each mate which he is not free to use in the counseling process without getting permission from the person who shared it. Respecting the confidentiality of material shared is fundamental to the trust level of the relationship, but it places the counselor in a tension situation when relating to the other partner.

Another problem of concurrent counseling is the possibility of being perceived by either of the counselees as more sympathetic to the other mate. In fact, there will be times when the minister is definitely more emotionally in tune with one or the other, but he needs to retain objectivity to function as counselor to both.

Concurrent counseling does have the value of allowing the individuals to speak freely about their feelings toward the mate, thus giving the minister opportunity to help them evaluate the appropriateness of such feelings and suggest possible ways of dealing with them.

(3) Conjoint counseling with both partners. Conjoint counseling involves seeing both persons in the marriage at the same time. The theoretical perspective of conjoint therapy is that the counselor gets the best picture of the systems operating in the relationship by seeing them interact with each other in the counseling room. Since the relationship is the patient, too, the nature of the interpersonal relationship can be understood better by seeing the couple conjointly.

Even though the scriptural passages seems to be referring to testimony in court, the word of Proverbs 18:17 is suggestive of the value of seeing the couple together: "He who states his case first seems right, until the other comes and examines him."

(4) Collaborative counseling. A less frequently used style of marital counseling is for the partners each to see separate counselors then for these counselors to collaborate with each other. It is always possible for the minister to refer people to a professional counselor with whom he keeps in contact, but this is not collaborative counseling in the technical sense. Ministers are seldom involved in this form of counseling, but it is still a possibility when couples will not see the same counselor.

Now that the four approaches have been described, it is important to recognize that the minister may combine these approaches while working with a marriage in trouble. He may want to see the couple together at the beginning of the counseling relationship, see them separately for a time, and then bring them back together in later visits. The conjoint method is recommended, however, when both partners are open to counseling help.

3. *Qualifications for Marital Counseling.* What personal characteristics contribute to success in marriage counseling? This question is important since research has demonstrated rather conclusively that the personality of the counselor is often more important to counseling success than the particular method or approach used by the counselor. This is not to infer that skill in dealing with interpersonal relationships is neither important nor necessary—skill development is essential for the minister. However, the way in which the minister relates to the people in acceptance and in creating an atmosphere of hope for change can be vitally related to fulfilling the task of helping troubled marriages become more satisfactory.

(1) A genuine love for people. Christian ministers, whether lay or clerical, can respond to human needs with the word of Paul giving them guidance: "Let us have no imitation Christian love" (Rom. 12:9, Phillips). Real love enables the counselor to enter deeply into the existential experiences of the couple so that they know someone else is available to help them bear the burdens of their struggle, but real love is not sentimentality.

"Sentimental love accepts the situation as the person himself describes it, and tries to find the remedy which he himself wants; and this may lead to all kinds of mistaken kindness," declared Samuel Shoemaker in his book, *How You Can Help Other People*. "Creative love has salt in it; it is very different from sentimental love."[6] David Augsburger calls this kind of love "caring enough to confront."

In its genuine willingness to confront, authentic love does not ride roughshod over the feelings of people. Empathetic concern is demonstrated in the tenderness exhibited by the counselor while encouraging people to indentify freely the hurts in their marriage. The apostle Paul, whom few would identify as unwilling to confront, described the nurturant quality of his love when he ministered to the Thessalonian believers, "But we were gentle among you, like a nurse taking care of her children. So, being affectionately desirous of you, we were ready to share with you not only the gospel of God but also our own selves, because you had become very dear to us" (1 Thess. 2:7-8).

(2) A good listener. Listening does not come easy to many of us in the preaching profession! Talking is our bread and butter; consequently, it is possible for us to talk too much and listen too little. The pressures of time may push us to give advice and directions to people before we have really heard and understood the nature of their relationship problems. Proverbs chastens us at this point: "If one gives answer before he hears, it is his folly and shame" (18:13).

A good listener is friendly, attentive, relatively shockproof, and alertly responsive to the communication being shared. Since communication is conveyed in nonverbal as well as verbal ways, the minister will be listening to the silent communication of body language along with the verbal language of the spoken word. This kind of attentive listening conveys to the counselee that his or her feelings are important and will be taken seriously by the minister.

Since faulty communication is basic to many marital difficulties, the minister can model the interactive quality of authentic listening and responsiveness as a way to help the couple learn how to increase the effectiveness of their own communication patterns. When the counselor responds understandingly to a statement made in the counseling interview, he may well hear, "Yes, that's what I mean! My wife (or husband) never seems to understand me like that."

(3) A reasonably well-integrated personality. Perfection eludes us all even though we may continually strive for it. The minister will be aided in helping other people, however, if self-awareness enables him to avoid letting such things as ungratified childhood impulses interfere with his ability to assist others. If married, the wholesome nature of his own marital relationship can be a part of this integration.

When the minister brings unresolved personality conflicts or marital dissension into the counseling experience, temptations to use people for personal fulfillment can occur. The minister who has never learned to handle personal anger may be unable to handle the anger one mate directs against another without condemning that angry feeling outright. If there is sexual frustration in the minister's own marriage, there can be an overidentification with a counselee who is having similar problems. When a woman is sexually hurting, male ministers have even been able to convince themselves that meeting her sexual needs through intercourse is for her good rather than for personal gratification! A healthy Christian personality is essential to good counseling.

(4) The ability to evaluate people. A minister must adopt an attitude of "sizing up" the people who come for help in order to help relate to their particular needs. Dr. Paul Pruyser of Menninger Clinic in Topeka, Kansas, is an active Christian layman who is a psychiatrist on the Menninger staff. In his book, *The Minister As Diagnostician,* he insists that more attention must be given to diagnosing difficulties rather than prescribing remedies without full awareness of what the remedy is supposed to be correcting. This evaluative perspective is important for increasing the effectiveness of counseling, and it is valuable in helping the minister avoid being used by people who seek his help. Not all people coming for counseling can be accepted at face value because there may be ulterior motivations for their participation.

On one occasion a couple came to the office at the wife's insistence. During the initial interview, the husband verbally voiced his willingness to participate in marital counseling, but he sat for the entire session with his back toward his wife. A couple of visits later, I told him, "You are wasting your money and my time. You don't have any desire to improve your situation."

His reply was direct and honest for the first time, "I don't like you, I don't like to come here, but as long as I keep coming she is easier to live with!" His nonverbal communication on the first visit was more authentic than his verbal assent, and he needed to be confronted about it.

4. *Methods of Marital Counseling.* The multiplicity of methods for marriage counseling available to the minister makes any categorizing of them very difficult in our limited amount of space. Distinctions are often made between directive counseling in which the counselor takes command of the interview and directs its process through leading questions and specific recommendations for action on the part of the counselees, nondirective counseling in which the responsibility for progress in the counseling relationship is dependent upon the ability of the counselee to lead the conversation, and some form of interactional counseling which engages counselor and counselee in a give-and-take interchange through the interview.

Application of these methods includes such approaches as behavior modification, learning theory, reality therapy, transactional analysis, integrity therapy, nouthetic counseling, and many others. In the midst of this diversity, it appears to me that two factors are important for the minister's choice of method. One, pastoral counseling, and particularly marriage counseling, will generally be eclectic. A counselor's methodology will usually draw upon a variety of sources without a commitment to one technique as applicable to every situation. Accepting this use of multiple sources as legitimate frees the minister to adapt method to situation.

Second, it is important for the minister to adopt some theoretical or philosophical framework within which the diversity can be more than grasping frantically at every new method proposed in some book on counseling. The framework should be consciously Christian in determining goals and objectives, but it should be psychologically sound as well in the use of established principles for helping people. The reading list at the close of this section is suggestive of resources describing different methods. Pastoral counselors who are sincere in their desire to aid troubled marriages will continue to study techniques and may also be able to complete supervised clinical experience to increase their competence in marriage therapy.

## Lay Support Systems

Churches are increasingly discovering that trained lay members offer great assistance in the counseling ministry to troubled marriages. Whether the ministry is provided through the official structures of the church, such as the Deacon Family Ministry plan of Southern Baptists or through couple-to-couple ministries under the direction of the minister or through group leadership for marital renewal, lay members can be effective counselors in the church.

During a sabbatical leave spent in England, I had opportunity to participate in the training activities of the National Marriage Guidance Council, an organization training laypeople for counseling in personal and marital difficulties. I was deeply impressed with the commitment to training and the caring response given by these men and women in their communities. They performed an excellent service to people in need.

J. C. Wynn points out that business people, homemakers, custodians, and other laypersons have been trained as family therapists, but so have young adults from the ghettos of Philadelphia. He concludes that a significant element in their success is "that they have learned to use themselves as genuine instruments of empathy and caring. They possess what envious professionals have come to refer to as 'factor X'—that is, affective empathy."[7] Churches can become involved in providing training or helping members locate training that capitalizes on that important "factor X."

## Remedial Marriage Retreats

A new approach to using group process in helping troubled marriages is a weekend retreat designed for therapy rather than enrichment. With the awareness that group participation can be a means of helping couples work through marital difficulties, the retreat is structured so as to focus on the stress factors of marriage rather than on the positive potentialities of marriage.

Most enrichment retreat leaders encounter one or more couples in a weekend experience who are really there for conflict resolution rather than enrichment. At times the small-group process on the retreat will be sidetracked as the group members try to deal with the problem couple in their group. The new approach would encourage couples having severe strain on their relationship to participate in a retreat where specific attention could be given to the emotional struggle they were encountering.

This method is too new to have any reportable evidence of success or failure, but it does offer churches a new direction for ministry to troubled marriages.

---

### Suggested Readings

Clinebell, Howard J. *Basic Types of Pastoral Counseling*. Nashville: Abingdon, 1966.

Collins, Gary R. *Christian Counseling*. Waco: Word Books, 1980.

Dale, Robert D. *A Pastor's Guide to Marriage Counseling*. Revised. Nashville: The Sunday School Board of the Southern Baptist Convention, 1982.

Drakeford, John W. *Counseling for Church Leaders*. Nashville: Broadman Press, 1961.

Glasser, William. *Reality Therapy*. New York: Harper and Row, 1965.

Hudson, R. Lofton. *Marital Counseling*. Englewood Cliffs, NJ: Prentice-Hall, 1963. (Interpersonal Competence Theory)

Knox, David. *Marriage Happiness: A Behavioral Approach to Counseling*. Champaign, IL: Research Press, 1971.

Oates, Wayne E. *An Introduction to Pastoral Care*. Nashville: Broadman Press, 1959.

Satir, Virginia. *Conjoint Family Therapy*. Palo Alto, CA: Science and Behavior Books, 1964.

Stewart, Charles W. *The Minister as Marriage Counselor*. Revised ed. Nashville: Abingdon, 1970. (Systems Theory)

# 6
# Growing Healthy Families

How would you describe a healthy family? The dictionary gives many definitions of *family,* but none of them really clarify for us what it is that we are trying to do in growing healthy families. Let me suggest one model for a healthy family that will introduce the educational and ministry needs of contemporary families.

First, the family is a place of commitment. Even though commitment in relationships has been downplayed in recent years, the Christian understanding of life demands relationships that can be counted on. The commitment is to love—the love of a man and a woman which begins the family through their own marriage, a love which includes physical attraction, friendship, and self-giving to need-meeting with one another, and a love which children may feel and give in return. The commitment is to faith—faith in one another as responsible persons who can be trusted to honor the marriage as a primary commitment which excludes other sexual involvements, faith that includes the decision to be cocreators of life in God's plan for the family, and faith in God's continuing presence in the home and family. The commitment is to hope—to believe that a future can be achieved with each other in which dreams and desires can be fulfilled through the contribution which each member of the family makes to its growth.

But the healthy family is also a place of potential conflict as individuals experience life at close quarters. A healthy family normally is not one free from differences in opinion and action but is one in which resolution of conflict nurtures growth. Conflict may occur between husband and wife, parents and children, median adults and their senior adult parents, as well as between brothers and sisters. It may produce anger, frustration, disappointment, rebellion, rejection, and hurt feelings; but conflict in itself need not destroy relationships. The key factor is effective and prompt resolution of conflict so that it will not cause internalized feelings to develop into resentment. A lesson in resolution of differences is fundamental in Paul's word concerning handling anger. "Be angry," said Paul, "but do not sin; do not let the sun go down on your anger, and give no opportunity to the devil" (Eph. 4:26-27). Accept the reality of the anger feeling, but don't let it deteriorate into resentment which can undermine the relationship.

Since a healthy family is one in which commitment and conflict can both be expressed, this means that it is also a place of challenge. Families are challenged to be places where every member of the family is encouraged to grow toward the maturity of personhood that God intends for them—the husband, the wife, the children, and the senior members of the larger family. Families are challenged to create environments within which fulfilling interpersonal relationships can develop. Families in Christian homes are challenged to make religion real by practicing their faith in the daily routine of the household. Families are challenged to grow in their spiritual, emotional, physical, and social fulfillments as they use available opportunity for family enrichment.

This model of a healthy family undergirds all that will be said in this chapter about the church's ministry to families. But we will also be looking at family from the perspectives of systems theory and the family life cycle.

Since the family life cycle was introduced in chapter 2, let us give brief attention to a significant contemporary theory about how families function.

The mother and step-father brought her teen-age daughter to the counseling center because she was creating so much stress in the home. As they entered the counseling room, the parents occupied the two chairs available. I started to get another chair for the girl but she said she wanted to sit on the floor close to my chair. The arrangement was like this:

Daughter X    X Counselor
Step-Father X         X Mother

After all were seated, the mother and step-father directed a stream of abuse at the daughter because of her behavior and because of her reported disrespect for her parents' wishes. She sat silently listening with tears running down her face.

After about fifteen minutes, I excused the parents in order to talk privately with the daughter. She acknowledged causing difficulties in the family even though she felt it was not as bad as they described it. Then it came out that her step-father was unhappy with her because she would not accept his suggestion that she wear fewer clothes around the house, especially when she completed her bath and went back to her bedroom to dress. He told her that he wanted her to feel good about her body, but she felt that he wanted to be able to see her body. Consequently she usually wore oversize clothes at home that completely obliterated her feminine characteristics.

When the daughter was excused and the parents returned, it soon became apparent that the wife was angry at her husband because of his interest in the daughter's body when he seemed to care little about hers. However, rather than direct her anger toward her husband, the mother directed her hostility toward the daughter and accused her of being the problem. This placed the daughter in a classic "double-bind" position— if she obeyed her step-father by wearing skimpy clothing at home, she would immediately be in conflict with her mother who would then yell at her rather than at her step-father.

This family illustrates some of the characteristics of the systems approach to family life. They had developed a system of response to one another which created continual turmoil in the home. When the daughter did not obey her step-father, he would get angry with the mother because her daughter was insubordinate. The mother could not take the daughter's side against her husband because of her own insecurity, so she would get angry with the girl. The daughter, angry because her mother was placing her in an untenable position, became argumentative and caused increasing trouble with her step-father. At the end of each episode, the girl would be punished, the father would often leave the house, and the mother would usually sulk. Time and again this system repeated itself in the home.

When the family came for counseling, the daughter was the "identified patient," the problem person. Actually the relationships within the triangle were the patients. The daughter was primarily the focus for the anger that the mother and step-father had for each other, and her anger was directed toward her mother for refusing to stand up for her, as well as at the step-father for what she felt to be sexually oriented feelings.

This family represents some of the concepts of systems theory described by J. C. Wynn in *Family Therapy in Pastoral Ministry*.[1] *Homeostasis* "suggests the equilibrium the family tried to keep, a balance that may be functional or dysfunctional, but one to which it has become accustomed." When we attempted to change the way the family was operating, it became necessary to clarify the relationship between the daughter's behavior and the parents' feelings toward each other. Dealing with those feelings was much more traumatic than continuing the pattern to which they had become accustomed.

Of course, homeostasis can work for the good of the family as well. Conflicts can be evaluated which threaten to disrupt the good balance of the family, and the homeostatic relationship of happiness can be recovered by resolving the conflict.

The *identified patient* is the one the family believes has the problem or is the problem. Family members have generally agreed that there is one person responsible for problems, and too often the person so described may accept the label as appropriate. Since the family members have concluded that the identified patient is the one who needs to be changed, "they will resist any new input that suggests their system of living has anything to do with the identified patient's problems."

A *double-bind* message is "a compulsorily confusing communication that cuts across two levels in a relatively contradictory style." In one situation, a woman came for counseling because of her inability to freely give affection to her children. In reflecting on her own childhood, there developed the picture of a mother who would verbally say "I love you" but who kept her physically at a distance when she wanted to put her arms around her mother. The double-bind message was "I love you but don't get close."

*Transcendence* reflects our earlier discussion of the whole being greater than the sum of its parts. The family system takes on a power of its own which resists change even though it is also characterized by *mutability*, the fact of constant and potential change. The minister counts on the capacity for change in working with ministry to families. *Equifinality* and *feedback* refer to the circularity of the family system. The same result in behavior can be attained by any number of approaches (equifinality), so the counselor is more interested in uncovering the system than just looking at the symptomatic problems. The feedback loop of information gained through experience, education, and therapy can be either positive or negative; but events affect families in a circular rather than a linear manner. All of these factors are a focus of *interpersonal relationships*, how the whole family interacts and affects each other.

There are other terms important to the full understanding of system theory; but this introduction helps us see that, just as the family is often the patient, the healthy family is also a source of strength to its members when the system operates for wholeness. Churches and ministers can help families discover how to change themselves within God's grace and power so as to produce healthy persons in life. This is both an educational and ministry function. Further attention will be given to this objective in chapter 7.

## Family Enrichment Activities

As pointed out earlier, family enrichment is different from marriage enrichment in its constituency rather than its direction. Family enrichment activities can include children, in-laws, grandparents, and singles as well as couples.

## Family Enrichment Conference

Preparing and conducting a Christian family enrichment conference is a new venture for many churches, but it is an increasingly popular feature of a church's ministry to its own members, as well as an attractive opportunity to invite people from the community to the church.

1. *Purposes.* Since the entire church family is involved in the conference, several purposes should be kept in mind when planning the program.

(1) One purpose is to provide an opportunity for a systematic presentation of Christian teachings on various aspects of family life. This is generally done in the assembly or worship period by the conference leader.

(2) Related to this is the purpose of providing a group forum or discussion period for considering pertinent family needs with suggestions for families to deal with those needs from a Christian perspective.

(3) A third purpose is to focus on the needs of single adults, whether never-married, widowed, or divorced, as an integral part of the church family. The divorced and the older widowed can sometimes feel that a family enrichment conference is not of interest to them unless the program planners place specific emphasis on their needs.

(4) The fourth purpose is to provide an opportunity to guide the thinking of youth toward a Christian understanding of dating, courtship, and marriage. Children's activities can emphasize home relationships and their part in creating a happy home.

2. *Length.* The most popular times for such conferences are Friday evening through Sunday night or Sunday through Wednesday night. Either of these time frames is an excellent program for Christian Home Week in May.

Some churches are devoting an entire month, such as May, to family enrichment activities using the regular meeting times on Sunday and Wednesday evening for the sessions. Columbia Baptist Church, Falls Church, Virginia, gives an entire month to the family emphasis with the minister's sermons, the music, worship services, and the training programs of conferences and seminars all centered on family.

3. *Daily Schedules.* The weekend plan usually begins on Friday evening with a meal for the entire family and continues through Sunday night with activities Saturday for selected groups, such as men, women, senior adults, youth. The entire family may be back for the Saturday evening program. The Sunday School and morning worship times are important periods of family life education and special activities may be planned on Sunday for singles, youth, children, or others. Singles often respond well to a luncheon after the morning worship.

The four-day program provides an opportunity for a different plan. Counseling can be provided by the conference leader(s) during the afternoons from about 2:00-5:00 o'clock with scheduled meetings from 7:00-7:50 for different age groups or interest groups. The 8:00 o'clock worship experience for the entire family may be a lecture or sermon, but it also is a time to celebrate what the Christian family can become. There is time during the week for special groups to meet for breakfasts, luncheons, or dinners during the four-day conference.

4. *Leadership.* The success of the conference will depend greatly on the quality of leadership enlisted for the general sessions and the group conferences. They must reflect good Christian character and be knowledgeable about the Christian understanding of family life. I recognize, of course, that some very competent persons may be used by the church who are not Christians in their religious orientation but who are sympathetic to the church's task in this vital area.

Competent leaders may be found among ministers, college and seminary professors, leaders in religious education in the churches, physicians, psychologists and psychiatrists, social workers, and public school teachers, as well as men and women in the church community.

5. *Finances.* Normally churches place an amount in their annual budget to care for the expenses of the family enrichment conference, including honorarium and expenses for visiting leaders. If the church plans to invite family life specialists, it is appropriate to ask them if they

have a regular fee schedule for conducting such programs. Clear understanding of the costs involved can save embarrassment for the church and the guests.

6. *Group Activities.* A number of approaches can be made to different age groups within the church family for the discussion periods. Preschool and younger children should have nursery and class provisions while the parents are in their sessions. These groups should remain in their own rooms for the entire evening so as to free the parents from child care responsibilities.

Older children can study selected materials on the home designed for their age group. These normally can be secured through denominational supply sources or from Christian book stores in the community. The children may come to the concluding worship experience, or they can remain in their own groups for the entire evening. Larger churches may provide a special worship service for the children.

Youth through adult groups may be organized by age groups or interest groups. The regular departmental divisions used in the church's educational program may be followed with youth, young adults, median adults, and older adults each having their own sessions with book study or conference leaders during the group discussion periods. The Southern Baptist Convention Equipping Center modules are an excellent resource for these discussions.

Adults and youth may be organized on an interest basis. These could include such discussions as: (1) dating and courtship, youth of junior and senior high; (2) preparation for marriage, youth engaged and/or seriously considering marriage; (3) adjustments in early marriage, couples who have been married for approximately one to five years; (4) the expanding family, growth of the family in numbers and responsibilities of parenting; (5) concerns of the aging family, such as adjustment to children leaving home, physical changes of aging, prospects of retirement; (6) singles, considering needs of those currently unmarried.

Combinations of these groupings could be used depending on the number of persons available for the various categories, as well as the church's access to available conference leadership.

7. *Program Suggestions.* A program of a four-day conference with a guest leader might include:

Sunday:     Sunday School—Adults and Youth—Understanding Christian Marriage

Morning Worship—The Christian Home in a Changing America

Evening Youth Discussion—The Urge to Merge

Evening Worship—Blueprint for a Christian Home

Monday:    6:30 AM—Men's Breakfast—The Man in the Mirror

Noon—Senior Adult Luncheon—Growing Old Gracefully

7:00 PM—Group Conferences

8:00 PM—Worship—Love Is No Luxury

Tuesday:    9:30 AM—Women's Coffee—Changing Roles of American Women

7:00 PM—Group Conferences

8:00 PM—Worship—The Miracle of Dialogue

Wednesday: 7:00 PM—Group Conferences

8:00 PM—Worship—The Church Confronting The Divorce Question

A weekend family enrichment conference could include:

Friday:     6:30 PM—Dinner for all ages—light entertainment—Home Is the Place

Saturday:   7:00 AM—Men's Breakfast—The Man in the Mirror

12:00 Noon—Senior Adult Luncheon—Growing Old Gracefully

7:30 PM—Family Worship—Love Is No Luxury

Sunday:     Sunday School—Adults and Youth—Understanding Christian Marriage

Morning Worship—Blueprint for a Christian Home

Noon—Single Adult Luncheon—Say Hello to Yourself

Evening Group—The Miracle of Dialogue

Evening Worship—When Your Children Disappoint You

The family enrichment conference provides a church with its most acceptable and widely focused type of enrichment experience. Individuals, couples, and families may each find a place of study and worship. Even though some churches reverse the order of worship and groups, it is my judgment that worship together is an excellent climax to the group discussion times.

The family enrichment conference also is a format adaptable to a multi-church emphasis in a local community or association of churches. A few years ago the Healing Springs Baptist Church in Virginia initiated a community conference in cooperation with the Bath County Ministerial Association. Four white and two black churches representing four denominations participated with day meetings at different churches and the evening services at the Healing Springs Baptist Church. Senior adults, businessmen, ministers, and adolescents had specific meetings but all the other sessions were designed to keep the family together for discussion, sharing, and planning. Under the theme of "Christian Family Living in Today's World," the conference focused on the centrality of love in family living—love of self, love of others, and love of God. Evaluations received after the conference commended the opportunity for crossing denominational and racial lines with this focus on the family.[2]

## Family Retreats

A family enrichment retreat takes the family out of its normal operating setting and transports it along with other church families to a camp or retreat setting where concentrated attention can be given to its needs and resources. When First Baptist Church, Huntsville, Alabama, offered such an opportunity, 43 families were represented on the retreat by 165 persons who attended. Henry Horton State Park near Nashville, Tennessee, was the site; the campers used tents, travel trailers, motor homes, and motel accommodations for housing their families. The three-day retreat included family worship, discussion groups, family recreation, and singing.

When the Woodmont Christian Church of Nashville, Tennessee, designed their family retreat, they planned both joint and separate group activities for parents, youth, and children. During the separate sessions, each age group dealt specifically with joys and problems in their own family situations. When the families were together, specific assignments were made to the families for exercises designed to help open up communication and set goals for their own families. Worship was a family affair with different families providing special music for the campfire and morning worship times.

An interesting exercise in family retreats is for each family member to list on a 3 x 5 card three things he or she likes about the family and one change that is desired. After each one completes the list, the individual families gather to hear from each member. No response, argument, or rebuttal can be given until all have shared their lists. Parents are often surprised at the positive feedback they receive from their teenagers, and the youth are sometimes surprised that parents really will listen!

Of course, listening is not always true. A card left by one youngster after such a session listed three positive things about his family and then graphically highlighted the need for change: Nobody listens to nobody!

Retreats can be designed that appeal to the camper spirit, but they may also be planned for retreat centers which provide motel-type accommodations for families. The latter is usually more expensive but are more desirable for people who do not like the camping routine for sleeping and eating.

## Audiovisual Programs

A popular type of family enrichment program is a series of film presentations which can be used as the basis for discussion among family members in the church setting. The James Dobson series, Focus on the Family, is one of the widely used series as is the Joyce Landorf series entitled His Stubborn Love. Using such a series of filmed presentations enables the church to bring in an expert presenter at a cost far below paying expenses and honorarium for such a leader and also provides material for discussion after the audiovisual presentation.

Some churches are missing the advantage of the films by not scheduling time for group discussion. This tends to make the films a performance rather than a learning experience since there is no opportunity for participants to hear one another or to solidify their own understanding by voicing it.

A vast array of family-related films, videotapes, and audiotapes are available through secular and religious sources. A word of caution must be said, however, about the use of these materials. Films or audiotapes should always be previewed before use. A film with an excellent rating for information may contain behaviors, language, or life-styles which will offend some particular users of the material. Advance previewing will enable the leader to know if the material should be used in the particular setting or whether adequate preparation of the hearers for these experiences will be sufficient to retain the valuable contributions of the material.

## Recreation

A substantial number of larger churches in the nation have built recreational buildings which often are called family life centers. Normally they contain facilities for recreational activities ranging from bowling, exercise rooms, racquetball, and basketball to swimming pools. The family life aspect of the center is that church family members have access as individuals or as families to the center within time guidelines established by the church.

Playing together is a valuable source of family unity. Someone has reworded the old cliche, "the family that prays together stays together" by having it read, "the family that prays *and plays* together will stay together." In the midst of our stress-laden and time-fractured society, playing together is one way that families rediscover their unity and enjoy their relationship.

Church programs of family recreation can include family fun nights in which family members compete against each other in games or families compete with other families. Children enjoy this kind of competition, and they also learn how to cooperate with their own family in inter-family competitions. In some activities, such as sports, some members play while other family members cheer them on.

The significant contribution of recreational planning is to make it as much a family affair as possible rather than always having the family divided up into age-related groups for the recreational activities.

---

**Suggested Readings**

Brown, S. Autry. *Church Family Life Conference Guidebook.* Nashville: Sunday School Board of the Southern Baptist Convention, 1973.

Christian, Esther. *Family Enrichment: A Manual for Promoting Family Togetherness.* Minneapolis: Educational Media Corp., 1982.

Edgren, Harry. *Fun for the Family.* Nashville: Abingdon, 1967.

Hart, Comp. *A Guide to Planning and Conducting a Retreat.* Nashville: Convention Press, 1977.

Hendrix, Lela. *Extended Family: Combining Ages in Church Experience.* Nashville: Broadman Press, 1979.

Koehler, George D. *Learning Together: A Guide for Intergenerational Education in the Church.* Nashville: Discipleship Resources, 1977.

LaNoue, John. *A Guide to Church Camping.* Nashville: Convention Press, 1976.

Otto, Herbert A., ed. *Marriage and Family Enrichment: New Perspectives and Programs.* Nashville: Abingdon, 1976.

---

## Family Workshops

Clearcut distinctions between workshops and other educational models, such as courses or seminars, are not always easy to make since the educational process in any one event may combine several approaches to learning. The word *workshop* in this section, however, describes a task-oriented program which involves the people themselves in research, action, and goal setting. The workshops to be discussed are intended to incorporate participation in accomplishing educational goals of learning by doing. Such workshops will often have leaders who have developed expertise in the particular field, but the leaders serve primarily as resource persons who guide the participants in their own study and practice.

Calling them *family workshops* implies two perspectives. In some instances, the workshops will focus on family needs and growth opportunities but will be offered to adults, youth, or children in sessions designed for their own age level and family responsibilities. In other cases the family can be involved in the workshop and will work with each other in accomplishing the objectives of the workshop. Churches are more familiar with the first style but can experiment profitably with the second. Let us look first at parenting workshops.

## Parenting Workshops

*Nobody Said It Was Easy* is not only the title of a book on parenting; it is also an experienced fact of parenting relationships! Christian parents are just as much involved in coping with the multiple demands of parenting as are people outside the church, so workshops on parenting are an important element of the church's family life education program. Since there are some factors in the Christian approach which are distinctive to the biblical understanding of life and parent responsibilities, let us briefly examine theological perspectives on children and parents.

1. *Theological insights.* There are three specific concerns in the parent-child relationship which I would like to consider. One is the nature of the child as sinner, the second is the meaning and purpose of discipline, and the third is parental responsibility for child guidance.

The spiritual condition of the child continues to surface in Christian interpretations of parent-child interactions, and the answer one gives to this question will affect the parental response to children's behavioral needs in the home. One tradition of the Christian community is that Adam's sin recorded in Genesis 3 continues to be ingrained in all children and that the parent must view misbehavior as an expression of sin rather than as human error. One writer identifies original sin in these words: "Automatically and inescapably from the very beginning of your existence you lacked faith and love and were inclined, instead, toward evil." Because of this influence of Adamic sin, "the newborn infant is guilty before God and under His wrath, not because he or she is being held responsible for someone else's wrong, but because he or she is corrupt."[3] In this tradition, corruptness will reflect itself in behavior, and parents must be alert to correct the evidences of sin in the child's life. The ultimate remedy for corruptness is in personal response to the forgiveness offered in Jesus Christ; therefore, parents must also be careful to direct the spiritual growth of their child toward conversion.

Related to this approach is the belief that the sins of the parents will manifest themselves in the children. For example, a publication of the Institute in Basic Youth Conflicts prepared for parents who adopt children emphasizes the inherited nature of sinfulness. The document affirms that "adopted children are affected by the sins of their *natural parents*, and these sins are usually very severe." Since adoptive parents need to be prepared to deal with sinful tendencies, they should find out all they can about the physical and spiritual weaknesses of the child's natural parents. Then, "based on these weaknesses, adoptive parents should set up clear and consistent disciplines for adopted children. They should explain that God wants them to be especially strong in these areas."[4] Areas of particular concern are spiritual sins of pride, lust, and rejection which may be inherited from the natural parents.

Fundamental to this approach is the understanding of total depravity as the virtual impossibility of human beings doing good in their natural state apart from faith in Christ. This interpretation of sin developed during the Protestant Reformation when sin was viewed as the innate corruption of the soul through the influence of Adamic sin which resulted in the total inability of the unsaved person to do good.

A different understanding of human nature after the fall is reflected in The Baptist Faith and Message adopted by the Southern Baptist Convention in 1963. Because of Adam's free choice to disobey God, "his posterity inherited a nature and an environment inclined toward sin, and as soon as they are capable of moral action become transgressors and are under condemnation." In spite of this reality, the image of God in humanity is not totally lost, and the sacrifice of Christ for all demonstrates that "every man possesses dignity and is worthy of respect and Christian love."[5]

This faith statement interprets total depravity (although the term is not used in the statement) in line with E. Y. Mullins's affirmation that it means "all the parts of our nature have been affected by sin . . . not that human nature is destitute of all good impulses in the moral sense . . . rather that human nature, as such, and in all its parts in its unregenerate state, is under the dominion of sin." Mullins, one-time professor of theology and president of The Southern Baptist Theological Seminary, applies this concept to children's spiritual condition in declaring that "the provisions of Christ's atoning work extend to them." The dominion of sin in their lives is demonstrated in the "facts of a hereditary bias to sin and of actual sin in all children as they become morally responsible." His conclusion is, therefore, that "men are not condemned for hereditary or original sin. They are condemned only for their own sins."[6]

From this perspective, the parent assumes the forgiveness of original sin until the child is old enough to comprehend the real nature of rebellion against God (cf. Rom. 3:23-25; 5:18-21). Alan Richardson, in A Theological Wordbook of the Bible, points out that the term original sin is not a biblical word but a human interpretation of the biblical portraits of sin which attempts to give a realistic description of human behavior. It describes what some theologians identify as the heart of sin—the human desire to put ourselves in place of God at the center of all things. Thus the "new-born infant comes into the world as the centre of his own universe, and all his education will consist in learning that he is not the centre of things." Richardson declares that, in dealing with so-called original sin, we must never forget the Original Righteousness that was man's in his creation in the image of God—an image which he has not lost completely in the fall. Because of that residual image, he is able to know his need for redemption and can respond in faith to the One who can reconcile him to his selfhood, to others, and to God.[7]

Discipline has often been equated with punishment, and there are numerous biblical references to punishment as a means of correctly rearing children (cf. Prov. 23:13-14; 22:15; 13:24). Unfortunately these passages have been used to condone punishment which actually becomes child abuse and has resulted in the death of children beaten by their parents. The New Testament portrait of God as Father made clear in the life of Jesus Christ does not support this interpretation of punishment even though physical punishment can be used effectively with younger children. However, the modeling effect of an adult physically administering punishment to a child can also create in the child a belief that it is all right to use force on persons whom they want to control. Spanking or other forms of physical control should be used sparingly.

The word *discipline,* however, means much more than punishment. It comes from the same root as the word *disciple* and connotes the idea of learning or training. Paul enjoined this larger meaning of discipline in his instruction to Christian parents to bring up children "in the discipline and instruction of the Lord" (Eph. 6:4). The word translated "discipline" in the context refers to the whole training and education of children in mental, emotional, and moral development. "Instruction" is the means by which this is done: exhorting, encouraging, admonishing. Phillips gives a good rendering of the entire verse in this translation: "Fathers, don't over-correct your children or make it difficult for them to obey the commandment. Bring them up with Christian teaching in Christian discipline."

Parental responsibility for child-rearing is already introduced by this Pauline reference, but it is constantly emphasized throughout the biblical revelation. A classic passage is Deuteronomy 6:4-9 in which parents are commanded to guide their children in knowledge and faith by the example of the parents' daily witness to God in the home. In the earlier Old Testament, the extended family suffered the consequences of parental sin, as can be seen in the experience of Achan (Josh. 7:16-26). In the later revelation through the prophets, children did not bear judgment because of their father's sins, but every child became responsible for personal transgression (Ezek. 18). Parental influence was and is certainly to be reckoned with in the home, but the sins of the parents are not visited on the children.

Parental responsibility included appropriate discipline, teaching, religious training, guidance in learning vocational skills, and care for the children in their needs. These qualities of child guidance have never been rescinded!

2. *Patterns of child-rearing.* Books on child-rearing are available by the hundreds, each having a particular perspective to guide parents in their task of rearing children. One of the consequences of this multiplicity of approaches is that many parents feel very insecure in their roles of disciplinarian, nurturer, chauffeur, friend, et cetera. Pediatrician W. Wayne Grant cites the lament of Johnny's frustrated mother when she brought him to the office for his eighteen-month checkup: "I'm afraid I'm going to do something wrong and ruin my child's life." Grant assured her that *one thing* would not ruin her child but he would be affected by the sum total of attitudes, actions, words, and behaviors of the parents toward him. As the church develops workshops in parent-child relationships, it will be concerned with basic philosophies of guidance rather than with specific behaviors.

As we examine patterns of child-rearing, I will use for a framework an interesting analysis of patterns of child guidance entitled *Parenting: Four Patterns of Child-Rearing.*[8] The authors recognize that different families will find different methods more suitable to their own inclinations and abilities, so they introduce four different methods with illustrative descriptions of each. They are convinced that parental values are central to the whole task of guiding children and devote the first chapter of the book to the "values that guide your parenting."

The first pattern is that of the "Potter." In this style, the parents take full responsibility and authority in the lives of their children in the conviction that parents determine what a child becomes. They are often active church members, have a strong sense of duty, and feel it their responsibility to interpret the children's feelings back to them since they usually are close to their children and know them well. The children are obedient, courteous, achievers, and have a keen sense of competition in their joy to achieve. The "Potter Parent" is a molder of children in the home.

Dr. James Dobson is representative of the persons who teach this style of parenting in the churches. In *Dare to Discipline* and *The Strong-Willed Child*, Dobson insists upon the children's need to know who the authority is in their lives if they are to learn how to live with each other and in society. He uses a strong biblical base for his approach to guidance. Illustrative of his position is his distinction between disobedience and rebellion. Young children disobey parents, and this can be corrected through guidance. When the young child rebels against parents, then parents must let him know who is boss and quell the rebellion!

The potter style requires strongly authoritative parenting even though it need not be (and should not be) merely authoritarian. The latter approach overwhelms the child's self-concept by denying the child's right to be a person whereas authoritative parents give guidance in a continuing respect for the selfhood of the child. It is a popular model with church groups because of its emphasis on parental authority.

Pattern two is the "Gardener." This style is founded upon the principles of developmental psychology. The parents believe that children develop into responsible youth and adults if given the chance and that they basically want to do so. Misbehavior occurs when natural growth and fulfillment are blocked. Stages of physical and emotional maturation contribute to the behavior patterns of the child, and these parents are alert to and understand the meaning of these stages. They seek to model acceptable ways of relating to others rather than impose rules, and they set limits for their children primarily with regard to safety and health. They believe children learn best when free to explore their own interests.

Pattern two children are usually open, unselfconscious, and verbal in their relationships with others. They tend to have good self-understanding because of the parental focus on developmental influences on selfhood, and they are often impulsive and assertive. The latter qualities are generally rewarding rather than problems in their interpersonal relationships.

A popular resource for the gardener style of parenting is *Child Behavior* by Frances L. Ilg, Louise Bates Ames, and Sidney M. Baker.[9] They are committed to the principle of physical and emotional maturation as the basic influence on childhood behavior. In their book they set out the various stages of development that children typically experience and point out the behaviors that can be expected by the parents at each stage. In this book they discuss children from birth to ten years of age, but another book by Ilg and Ames discusses the years from ten through sixteen.

Other important figures in this style of child understanding are Erik H. Erikson, to whom reference was made in previous chapters, and Selma Fraiberg in *The Magic Years*. Within the Christian community, *Growing Parents Growing Children* by W. Wayne Grant focuses on the developmental approach to understanding children and has goals similar to the gardener style of parenting.

"The Maestro" is descriptive of the third pattern of child-rearing. These parents are goal oriented with high standards for themselves and their children. They assume their challenge is to provide a carefully planned social and physical environment in which their children can learn and grow and solve problems. Believing in the democratic tradition, they take pride in the group achievement by their children but also protect each family member's need for a personal life as well as a family community life. They study parenting skills and are ready to assign responsibilities as soon as their children are ready to accomplish them. In that sense they represent some of the characteristics of pattern two developmental philosophy.

Children in these families tend to be competent and, therefore, feel competent because their parents have taught them to do well the things they undertake. They have a strong need to achieve, learn the acceptable ways to do things, are organized, productive, and reliable.

The Systematic Training for Effective Parenting (STEP) program appears to be illustrative of training material for pattern three parenting. In its affirmation of social equality for parents and children and its belief that misbehavior communicates a felt need of children, STEP is in line with the discussion of this style of parenting.

*Peoplemaking* by Virginia Satir is another resource for the maestro model of parenting.[10] Satir describes the family as a factory within which mature human beings are developed out of children. The parents are "the *people-makers.*" She centers her discussion of how parents go about the task of developing persons around the four themes of self-worth, communication, rules people use for how they should feel and act, and the way family members relate to people and institutions outside the home. Her book is filled with exercises that can be adapted for workshop use in the church even though it is not designed as a religiously-oriented resource.

Perhaps the most relevant biblical reference to pattern three parenting is "train up a child in the way he should go,/and when he is old he will not depart from it" (Prov. 22:6) although the developmental concept of Christian maturing is also applicable to this approach.

Pattern four is characterized as the "Consultant." These parents work hard at knowing and accepting themselves as responsible parents and regard their children and themselves as constantly growing and learning about relationships. They relate to their children in a manner similar to the way they relate to their peers and do not see themselves as ultimate authorities for their children. Because they adopt goals in child-rearing rather different from some of their neighbors or friends, they don't worry too much about what other people think about their methods.

Children of pattern four parents tend to be creative, independent thinkers with highly developed imaginations and may be considered nonconformists by other parents. They are not always unquestioningly obedient, even though they are normally reliable and sensitive to the feelings of other people.

*Parent Effectiveness Training,* the name of a book and a program by Thomas Gordon, is probably the best-known representative of the pattern four workshops.[11] Gordon repudiates the parent-power approach to child guidance in favor of mutual decision-making among equals. His "no-lose" method of parent-child relationships resolves conflicts by finding solutions mutually acceptable to parent and child through parent-child dialogue. Since the child participates in the decision, he is motivated to carry out the solution rather than rebel against parental power which forces a decision on him. This approach, says Gordon, develops children's thinking skills, encourages more love and less hostility, requires less enforcement by parents, and gets to the real problems of misbehavior or resistance. It is based upon treating children in an adult fashion to which they respond by feeling trusted and capable.

Even though some religious leaders resist P.E.T. because they believe it undermines the God-given authority of parents over children, a number of churches have found this a valuable resource for parental training. Dr. Dale Keeton, of Columbia Baptist Church in Virginia, became a certified instructor in the program and has taught the eight-week, twenty-four hour program to over a thousand church people since 1972. He points out that "while the program is in no way a cure-all, we found that the experience in our parent training program offered not only tools in the form of skills but also encouragement to many who were struggling with the challenging task of parenting."[12]

The authors of *Parenting: Four Patterns of Child-Rearing* provide much more data on the principles and limitations of each style which can be helpful to church leaders in planning their own programs. The valuable contribution they make is to give churches a resource by which to identify the styles of parenting that the leadership desires to implement in the church and community and suggest methods for doing it.

An additional value of this examination of parenting is that the approaches can be used in workshops for all types of parenting situations: traditional two-parent homes, single parent situations, and blended families. Resources for each of these family needs are included in the reading suggestions on the next page.

### Family Worship Workshops

"Family worship? That's a lost cause in this busy age," declared a mother of three children when a workshop on family worship was proposed for her church. "If you could see the harried schedules we all have every day you would realize that we could never plan time to be together every day to have a devotional activity."

Research into families in the churches gives credence to this mother's lament. A 1962 survey of youth in The Lutheran Church-Missouri Synod revealed that although 72 percent of them were regular church

---

**Suggested Readings**

Two-Parent Families

Blackwell, William and Muriel. *Working Partners/Working Parents.* Nashville: Broadman Press, 1979.

Cooper, John C. *Living, Loving and Letting Go: The Art of Being a Parent.* Waco: Word Books, 1977.

Duvall, Evelyn. *Handbook for Parents.* Nashville: Broadman Press, 1974.

James, Muriel. *What Do You Do with Them Now That You've Got Them?* (Transactional Analysis for Moms and Dads). Reading, Mass.: Addison-Wesley, 1974.

Single Parent Families

Bel Geddes, Joan. *How to Parent Alone: A Guide for Single Parents.* New York: Seabury, 1974.

Gatley, Richard H. and Koulack, David. *Single Father's Handbook.* Doubleday: Anchor Books, 1979.

Jones, Eve. *Raising Your Child in a Fatherless Home.* London: Collier-Macmillan, 1963.

Stewart, Suzanne. *Parents Alone.* Waco: Word Books, 1978.

Blended Families

Berman, Claire. *Making It as a Stepparent.* Garden City: Doubleday, 1980.

Berman, Eleanor. *The Cooperating Family.* Englewood Cliffs: Prentice-Hall, 1977.

Duberman, Lucile. *The Reconstituted Family: a Study of Remarried Couples and Their Children.* Chicago: Nelson-Hall, 1975.

Maddox, Brenda. *The Half-Parent: Living with Other People's Children.* New York: M. Evans & Co., 1975.

---

attenders, only 19 percent were participants in any form of regular family worship experiences. Estimates among Southern Baptists suggest that only 5 to 10 percent of the families have any type of regular devotional periods. In spite of these reports, families surveyed by Southern Baptists in 1978 expressed a real need for help in establishing family worship. Forty-five percent of the husbands and 40 percent of the wives listed this as one of the three most serious needs of the family. Both husbands and wives listed a family worship workshop as the family

ministry project most needed in their churches. Churches are challenged by the figures to find new ways of encouraging family worship
among their people. Both the Bible and human experience testify to the
value of worship in the home.

## Biblical Illustrations of Family Worship

Attention has already been given to the Deuteronomic exhortation for
families to experience a deepening appreciation for God's word in the
home when the parents teach his commandments diligently and talk of
them during the daily activities of family life (Deut. 6:4-9). Significant
allusions to family interaction in worship are found in the events of the
Exodus. After the first Passover in Egypt, the Israelites were commanded
to keep the Passover as households in remembrance of their deliverance.
At the Passover time, when "your son asks you, 'What does this mean?'
you shall say to him, 'By strength of hand the Lord brought us out of
Egypt, from the house of bondage'" (Ex. 13:14). A similar situation
developed after the crossing of the Red Sea. Joshua appointed one man
from each of the twelve tribes to take a stone from the Jordan River bed
and erect a marker on the shore. Then he said, "When your children ask
their fathers in time to come, 'What do these stones mean?' then you
shall let your children know, 'Israel passed over this Jordan on dry
ground'" (Josh. 4:21-22). The children's questions became a regular part
of family worship rituals among the Hebrew people.

Families worshiped in the Temple and synagogues even though men
were separated from women in these religious settings. In the New
Testament, the young churches met in homes after being put out of the
Jewish houses of worship. Since families rather than individuals were
central to Jewish thought in their worship experiences, the Bible affirms
the desirableness of family worship at home and in the churches.

## Universal Encouragement of Family Worship

Virtually all religious communities emphasize the value of family
worship for their constituents. Oscar E. Feucht of the Missouri Synod
Lutheran Church maintained that "no other single custom in the

Christian home contributes so much to keeping it functionally Christian."[13] An American Baptist publication declared that the modern family "needs to center its life on God, if it is to have any center of meaning and any source of strength beyond itself,"[14] and this centering is reinforced by family worship experiences. These are but two samples of the genuine acclaim given to family worship by different faiths and denominations.

Unanimous acclaim, however, has not always fostered the development of training opportunities which can help families gain a perspective on home worship in our busy world and teach them how to go about it. This is the challenge facing family ministry in this vital area.

## Objectives of Family Worship

What is it we are trying to accomplish in fostering workshops on family ministry? It appears to me that we can focus on several objectives for families as they continue or begin some form of regular home worship. I will simply list the objectives without discussion:

(1) experiencing God's presence in the joys, sorrows, and struggles of daily life;

(2) growing in their understanding of the Bible as the communication of God's word to his people;

(3) strengthening families to meet crises more effectively by relying upon the Bible and upon God's grace through prayer;

(4) developing moral values through study of and application of biblical teachings for personal and social life;

(5) helping families practice the Christian graces of love, forgiveness, patience, and understanding with each other.

## Model for a Family Worship Workshop

Southern Baptists adopted as one of the goals for their 1982-1985 emphasis on Strengthening Families an objective of enlisting 500,000 additional families in family worship. As one of the training resources for this emphasis, an Equipping Center module was developed on *How to Lead Your Family in Bible Study and Worship*. The kit includes a short filmstrip introducing the module, a booklet for each individual or family containing the basic information for discussion, a leader's guide for group discussion of the material, and a guide for individual study if a person desires to study the module alone.

This material can be used in an individual church, or it can be the focus of training for a group of churches. However, it can also be used by any family that desires to explore the possibilities of family worship activities in their own family. The module is available through Baptist Book Stores.

In whatever models are developed for training families, three principles may be important for contemporary family life. One, there is no set method which every family needs to follow. Worship is inclusive of music, prayer, meditation, Scripture, inspirational readings, nature walks, fun times, and other experiences of normal family life. Discourage boredom by varying the method.

Two, there is no best time although a set time is valuable for scheduling. It may be daily, weekly, or on some other time schedule but each family needs to consider the best time for its own situation. Family type or stage of the family life cycle will also dictate something about scheduling. Third, all family members who are old enough should share in the leadership of the worship times and help in choosing the resources used. This may mean that teenage children will prefer a different style of music for worship than middle-aged parents but, if the experience is to be truly a family one, they need to have freedom to choose. Cooperative involvement contributes to success.

---

**Suggested Readings**

Elder, Carl A. *Values and Moral Development in Children*. Nashville: Broadman Press, 1976.

Gebhard, Edward W. and Anna Laura. *Guideposts to Creative Family Worship*. New York: Abingdon-Cokesbury, 1963.

Herring, Reuben. *Your Family Worship Guidebook*. Nashville: Broadman Press, 1978.

Whitehouse, Donald S. and Nancy S. *Pray and Play: A Guide for Family Worship*. Nashville: Broadman Press, 1979.

## Money Management Workshops

Marriage counselor and family specialist Dr. David Edens rightly points out that "money is a vital force in nearly every facet of a couple's life no matter what the income level. More waking hours are spent earning money than doing anything else, and the couple's entire life style is tied to the pattern of earning and spending it."[15] Marriage counselors are reporting that many couples who have been having difficulties for years are now seeking counseling because their poor economic situation during inflationary times has aggravated problems they had long ignored. But money management is not only a concern for married couples. Single adults and formerly married make up over fifty percent of the population of the United States and they, too, have money management problems. Since it is common for singles and couples alike to have had little training for dealing with the complexities of handling money appropriately, money management workshops can meet a real need in family ministry.

## Attitudes Toward Money

Contrary to the popular opinion that more money would solve all problems, one of the first factors influencing the use of money is one's attitude toward it. Three words may be used to describe possible attitudes: selfishness, symbolic, and stewardship. The selfish use of money focuses on one's own needs and desires for money or possessions and an unwillingness to share responsibly with others in the family. We have all seen the child who vehemently refuses to share with other children, and this same attitude may surface in family relationships. Either husband or wife may be the one, but it is usually the income producer who claims it for personal use. The influence of sin in human life can be seen graphically when money is viewed selfishly!

However, the symbolic attitude toward money is more universal and more conducive to family friction than is pure selfishness. In this perspective, money is viewed in terms of its emotional meaning rather than as a medium of exchange. William Kaufman describes this attitude as psychosomatic "money-sickness." The use of money is shaped by the conscious (or unconscious) desire to fulfill emotional attitudes including the emotionally well-balanced use of money which creates in the individual a sense of well-being and emotional security; the compulsive nonspender for whom money represents love, affection, and security which was denied during growing up years, thus the desire to hoard it; the compulsive spender who seeks to gain friendship and acceptance by spending money; the fearful user of money who may buy a product in order to please the salesperson—whether a car or after-shave lotion; and the use of money as a reward which can manipulate the behavior of others constructively or destructively.[16] An irrational fear of money itself and the problems of controlling it can be part of this emotional attitude toward money.

Susan Bondy, at twenty-four years of age, had a deep-seated fear of finances. Her bankcard bill grew every month until the finance charges were embarassing. Her monthly bank statement simply told how much she had borrowed against her overdraft protection. She had a few dollars in savings, but said of herself at that time, "I was paralyzed." Interestingly enough, her daily job was doing risk analysis for pension funds in an investment firm! She said, "I knew all the right strategies, but I couldn't bring myself to use them." Her fear of handling money for its intended use kept her from dealing forth-rightly with her money problems. This same Susan Bondy is now a financial consultant giving lectures to laymen and business people alike in ways to handle money appropriately. She overcame her fear and now handles money differently.[17]

Stewardship is the third attitude possible for money management. In the approach, money is recognized as a servant and not a master. Jesus pointed to this attitude when he declared that "no one can serve two masters; for either he will hate the one and love the other, or he will be devoted to the one and despise the other. You cannot serve God and mammon. . . . For where your treasure is, there will your heart be also." (Matt. 6:24,21). The stewardship attitude views all of one's possessions as a trust from God to be used responsibly and in accord with God's purpose for life. It includes not only one's support for Christian causes but it also applies to the way the total income of the person or family is used. Authentic stewardship frees a person to deal honestly and competently with family income problems. Selfish or symbolic uses of money make money management more difficult because self-concept issues are involved.

## Models of Money Management Workshops

*Christians Doing Financial Planning,* a workbook developed by the Commission on Stewardship of the National Council of Churches, includes an excellent guide to a workshop for families or groups desiring to improve their financial management. Four sessions of one hour or more are suggested for the study with the first session devoted to New Testament insights about stewardship. Personal and family values about money and their importance in the way money is spent are considered in the second session with sharing of factual information to help individuals or families plan money use more effectively in the third session. The last session is actual practice in budget preparation for the individual or family using a case study approach. The manual includes resource material for each of these sessions with guidelines for the group leader to use in teaching the material.

The Interfaith Council for Family Financial Planning, a program of the American Council of Life Insurance in Washington, D.C., has cooperated with denominational leadership to develop workshops for financial planning. In cooperation with the U.S. Catholic Conference of Bishops, for example, pilot projects were completed focused on couples, on families, and for single women. Resource materials are available from ACLI for church workshops.

Southern Baptists have workshop models available through their Baptist Sunday School Board as well as the Annuity Board of the Southern Baptist Convention. *A Christian's Guide to Financial Planning* is one of the Equipping Center modules for individual, family, or group use. Designed for six sessions, it deals with biblical backgrounds for stewardship, attitudes toward money management, and budget planning guidelines. The Annuity Board publication *Christian Family Money Management* is a packet of materials to guide families, as well as individuals, in budget preparation and money management.

Financial planning and money management workshops need to include such areas as two-income family needs, single adults with particular reference to single women, legal factors such as preparing a will, single parent concerns, and the relationship of children in the home to money matters.

---

**Suggested Readings**

Bergler, Edmund. *Money and Emotional Conflicts.* 2nd ed. New York: International Universities Press, 1972.

Fooshee, George. *You Can Be Financially Free.* Old Tappan, NJ: Revell, 1976.

Household International. *Money Management Booklet Library.* (A series of 12 booklets) Prospect Heights, Illinois.

Speer, Michael L. *A Complete Guide to the Christian's Budget.* Nashville: Broadman Press, 1975.

Schurman, Paul G. *Money Problems and Pastoral Care.* Philadelphia: Fortress Press, 1982.

# 7
# Ministering
# to Family Needs

Family needs are generally considered from two different perspectives: developmental and accidental or crisis. Developmental needs are natural to the developmental cycle of family life, whereas crisis needs are related to unexpected events which place unusual demands for coping on the individuals or families involved. Family ministry seeks to provide pastoral care by the minister and the congregation to both kinds of needs. In this chapter, we will examine some new approaches to pastoral care and then review ministry possibilities in crisis situations.

## Pastoral Care

The phrase *pastoral care* has traditionally described the care given to church members by vocationally trained ministers, such as pastor, associate pastor, or others. The word *pastoral* comes from the Greek word describing the work of a shepherd and was used by Paul to identify one category of gifts for ministry which God gives to the church. He declared that God's "gifts were that some should be apostles, some prophets, some evangelists, some pastors and teachers, to equip the saints for the work of ministry, for building up the body of Christ" (Eph. 4:11-12). In this translation, the pastor-teacher role is combined into the functions of equipping and ministering. Other translations clarify the purpose of the minister's calling, however, in a way that is more faithful to the Greek text.

The *Good News Bible,* for example, translates it: "He did this to prepare all God's people for the work of Christian service, in order to build up the body of Christ" (v. 12). Phillips makes it even clearer, "His gifts were made that Christians might be properly equipped for their service, that the whole body might be built up." In these translations, the work of the pastor-teacher is to do ministry but also to equip members of the congregation for their own ministry to each other.

Based largely upon the influence of the Ephesian letter, pastoral care has come to be understood from two perspectives: (1) the ministry of the vocationally called minister and (2) the care exercised by the congregation to one another. We will discuss family counseling as one aspect of vocational ministry and lay caregiving as the ministering function of the congregation.

### Family Counseling

The telephone rang about 8:30 P.M. as Pastor Raymond Green was relaxing in the family room of his home. "Pastor, our daughter has been picked up by the police for shoplifting," said the anguished parent. "Can you come over to the house to help us decide what to do?"

This cry for family counseling by the pastor highlights one meaning of the term. It is pastoral counseling of family members in times of developmental or crisis stress. The minister may see part of the family or all of it during the course of counseling with them, but he may not feel impressed to bring the whole family into the counseling situation at one time. Most of the literature related to pastoral care of families provides guidance in doing this kind of family counseling.

If, however, Pastor Green decides that the daughter's shoplifting is related in some way to the functioning relationships in the family, or if the family determines to make her the "identified patient," he may choose to deal with the family as a whole. This is the newest form of family counseling and is usually called family therapy. Family therapy was introduced in chapter 6 in the discussion of family systems theory. Now let us examine how this type of therapy might work in actual practice.

1. *Develop your approach.* Douglas A. Anderson defines pastoral family therapy as "an organized, purposeful therapeutic intervention aimed to assist a family to change—under the power of the Holy Spirit."[1]

Since family therapy requires greater attention to power structures, interpersonal feelings, and family gamesplaying, the minister planning to use this methodology should prepare himself through study and possible clinical training to engage in it. Having a general understanding of how healthy families operate and how dysfunctional families block out growth is important in determining what the minister wants to accomplish in the sessions.

2. *Assume responsibility for leading the sessions.* In contrast to nondirective styles of counseling, the family therapist is an active participant in the actions taking place in his study. Even though the family has already tried to deal with their problem situation and failed, the tendency is for them to continue trying the old methods and relationships. The minister is the person who directs the interviews rather than letting the dominant family members do so. This firm leadership is a significant key to change in the family system.

3. *Identify with the family.* All family therapists emphasize identification with the family as basic to the process. This requires the establishment of trust, but if the minister is known to the family, trust may already be implicit in their coming to him. In becoming a family member temporarily, various therapists use different methods of involving themselves with the family members. Some use the technique called *sculpting* which involves physically placing family members in positions that illustrate how any family member might experience the others in the family and then place them the way he or she would like to experience them. A simple illustration would be for a child to place parents in positions facing away from her and then turn them to face toward her as indication of her need to be recognized in the family setting.

At times a therapist will form an alliance with one family member and together they confront the rest. In many ways the family therapist enters into the drama of the family for the purpose of helping the family see itself in its functioning. Even if there is not physical joining of it, the process of therapy demands an active role rather than a passive role to effect change.

4. *Discover the problem(s).* After the family has been greeted and seated

in the first interview, a common technique is for the therapist to ask each family member to describe what he or she believes to be the problem in the family. Other members are not allowed to break in or speak for the one who is talking regardless of the age of the person. This allows the minister to gain a perspective on what the family is experiencing from the children as well as the adults, and it avoids joining in the possible identification of the "identified patient" by beginning with that person.

Wynn believes that it is important to balance this discussion of problems by inviting the family to tell about the strengths and happy times they have had. Each person is invited to share this time of affirmation.

Having an interpretation of family problems from all of the family gives the minister a beginning handle on what is happening in the family system. Normally the next step is to determine what moves the family has already made to cope with or overcome the problems they are having. In order to deal with change, the minister will want to know what has not worked well even though it may have been the traditional or system way of handling problems in the past.

Based upon this diagnostic procedure, the minister will begin to develop a tentative assessment of the family's interactional problems. This part of family therapy is crucial because it will determine what kind of interventions the minister believes can be used to break into the system and move them toward change.

5. *Determine change possibilities.* Here again the involvement of the family is significant. When they are asked individually to suggest what changes are possible or desired, parents are sometimes shocked at the suggestions made by their children. The therapist assists the family in evaluating what changes they want instead of assuming that he can tell them what to do or let them make him bear responsibility for telling them what they should do.

6. *Contract for change.* By the time of the third or fourth interview, the minister should be able to guide the family in developing a contract for change that becomes their working agreement. As Wynn points out, "if the family is ever to make a positive alteration in their system they will have to carry it on themselves."[2]

Ministers may expect to encounter more opposition from the family when they get to this stage of therapy. The homeostasis described in chapter 6 must now be disturbed by the intervention of the minister into the working pattern of the family, and such change is seldom welcomed wholeheartedly even though the family came for counseling. In spite of this resistance, the working out of a specific contract for change is the most promising part of the therapy. Since change is related to behaviors rather than attitudes, concrete plans that the family can implement and report on are essential to this type of approach.

7. *Maintain focus on family responsibility for change.* By having the family members report on the implementation of their contracted agreement and refusing to accept excuses easily, the minister helps the family remain at the center of the healing process. Assignments are reviewed in the counseling sessions, and new directives are given that will keep the family working on its new pattern of functioning. Since dysfunctional families often seek a cause for their problem in something or someone outside of the family, the minister may become the scapegoat for their failure to improve unless constant attention is directed to the family system.

8. *Prepare the family for termination of therapy.* The ultimate goal of the therapist is for the family to deal with its own problems in a new way, thus preparation for termination of the interviews is a significant part of the process. In general family therapy is considered short-term, with an average of six to seven visits to the therapist. Since the focus is on present behavior rather than insight development or attitude change as a primary aspect of therapy, families can be encouraged to become self-reliant through behavior change more quickly.

This brief review of how family therapists approach their task introduces a very rewarding type of family counseling which ministers are often ideally suited to use. In an average congregation, the minister is usually acquainted with the family members and may be able to use insights into the family system drawn from interaction with the extended family of grandparents and others, as well as the family seeking help. Having the family in therapy exposes more emotional nerves than does conjoint marriage counseling where the minister is relating to a couple, but it builds upon the same strengths of such counseling.

---
**Suggested Reading**

Anderson, Douglas. *New Approaches to Pastoral Care*. Philadelphia: Fortress, 1980.

Bandler, Richard, Grinder, John, and Satir, Virginia. *Changing with Families*. Palo Alto, Calif.: Science and Behavior Books, 1976.

Hoffman, Lynn. *Foundations of Family Therapy: A Conceptual Framework of Systems Change*. New York: Basic Books, 1981.

Wynn, J. C. *Family Therapy in Pastoral Ministry*. San Francisco: Harper & Row, 1982.

---

## Lay Caregiving

The pastor of a suburban Saint Louis church decided to equip some laymen for pastoral care in order to spread the load of meeting people's needs to more people. He chose three retired men who had time for training and for actual practice of ministry. They accompanied him on evangelistic visits, hospital calls, and visits to families at home. Their response to the new use of their Christian gifts was tremendous.

On one occasion, the pastor and one layman called upon a young Baptist minister in a local hospital. The minister's baby son was dying from an incurable disease which had been a problem since birth. There was no insurance. Debts from the time of the baby's birth were still hanging over the family, and now hospital bills were growing again. In fact, the hospital business office had been confronting the couple for some payment of past bills.

After praying with the young minister, the pastor and layman moved on toward their car. Then the layman exclaimed, "Pastor, I want to help that young couple if I can. I'm going back to his room for a moment to ask his permission to do so." When the permission was gladly given by a grieving father, the layman went to work.

He first contacted the administrator of the Roman Catholic hospital and alerted her to the situation. She did not know of the troubled family's plight but agreed to see if the hospital could do anything to help out. From there the layman went to a Jewish funeral director and explained the family's impending need for funeral services and that they were without funds to pay for it. The funeral director offered his services free of charge except for the $75.00 necessary for opening the grave. Leaving the funeral home, the layman got in touch with his own Sunday School class for assistance with food and other necessities.

When he again contacted the hospital administrator, she had found that some money was available from a crippled children's organization and that the hospital could absorb some of the bill as a charitable contribution. These sources reduced the family debt from over five thousand dollars to slightly under two thousand dollars.

Through all of this activity, the layman continued to minister to the family and was on hand when the baby died. In every way, this layman was fulfilling a pastoral care approach to lay caregiving.

Most of the literature on equipping laypeople for caregiving has been written in the last ten years, yet almost forty years ago Samuel L. Shoemaker wrote *How You Can Help Other People* as a guide for lay members of the church in addition to ministers. He asked, "How far can a layman be expected to do this delicate and difficult work?" Answering his own question, Shoemaker declared, "It all depends upon how much he wants to do it, and will therefore give time and study, so that he may learn enough to make him effective." Writing against the backdrop of the end of World War II, he believed that "the need today is of such proportions that professionals cannot be had in sufficient numbers. . . . The clergy ought to be foremost in the ranks of those who do this work, and they ought to train their lay people to do it."[3]

Increasingly since 1946 ministers have become accepted as caregivers, and this has increased the need for heeding Shoemaker's advice about training laypeople for this task. However, ministers who decide to equip lay members for pastoral care will find some obstacles to overcome if the work is to be done effectively.

Some of the resistance will be internal, in the minister's own self-concept and need for affirmation. Ministering to the hurts of the congregation is what seminary trained him to do. Hospital calls, marriage and family counseling, crisis intervention—these are what ministry is all about. Equipping others to do that may feel like giving up an arm or leg! Another difficulty is that performing such ministry to persons in need is one of the most direct means by which the minister receives personal affirmation from church members. He will not hear that ego-boosting word, "O pastor, I appreciate so much the help you have been to me during this illness. I know that you are *so busy,* but you came to see me!" If laypeople are trained to do pastoral care, people will not be acclaiming the minister for selecting and equipping these laypeople, they will give that acclaim to the ministering person.

On the other hand, resistance may come from the congregation. Lacking an authentic New Testament understanding of shared ministry, members may declare, "Our pastor is really trying to get out of work by getting all these members to do what we pay him to do!" Others may not be willing to accept the ministry of laypersons as officially representative of the church's concern for them. Pastoral care to them must always be given by the vocational staff if it is really *pastoral* care. It may also be true that members may resist accepting responsibility for pastoral care even though they have accepted the roles of teacher, secretary, recreational director, cook, and a host of others.

Educating a congregation to accept its responsibility to minister to each other requires, therefore, that the minister examine his own willingness for others to receive acclaim instead of himself. It also requires an extended period of preparation for inaugurating such a program and a specific training program for those who are willing to assume this new task. Available evidence from churches that have undertaken this approach indicates that it can and does work. In some cases it is done through official church structures and in others it may be person to person or family to family.

1. *Through official structures.* Lay caregiving has been done in an unrecognized way for many years through Sunday School classes and departments. I remember when my wife's mother was president of her senior adult class and called upon group leaders to report on their absent members. Each group leader was expected to be in contact with

her group, share any particular needs with the class, and personally visit the member who was ill or had some other need for concern. These ladies would not have called what they were doing pastoral care, but it was a form of congregational caregiving through the regular Sunday School activities.

An excellent example of lay caregiving is the Deacon Family Ministry Plan of Southern Baptists. In that denominational ecclesiology, deacons are lay members who traditionally were male and served as an official board of the church with responsibility for business affairs and sometimes for reviewing all matters brought to the floor of the congregational business meeting. In recent years, however, deaconship has taken a new direction under the leadership of the church administration staff of the Baptist Sunday School Board. Emphasis is now placed on the meaning of *diakonos* as servant rather than board member, and deacons are being chosen and trained as ministers to the congregation. Henry Webb, in *Deacons: Servant Models in the Church,* says, "The purpose of this book is to help deacons to demonstrate in their lives and to apply in their churches the biblical concepts of their role as servant leaders." He then declares that "the New Testament model of service and today's need point to deacons serving alongside the pastor in pastoral ministries."[4]

In the family ministry plan for deacons, church members who are assigned to individual deacons become essentially the small flock of a shepherding person. The deacon is expected to visit them in their homes and is available to minister to them at times of joy, such as the birth of a baby, or in sorrow, such as the death of a family member. Perceptive visiting permits the deacon to become aware of family needs that may be brought to the attention of the pastor or other staff members. Deacons are encouraged to send cards on birthdays and notes when opportunities come for such remembrances. In every way possible, church members are led to know that the deacons care for them.

Resources for training deacons during retreats and sessions at the church are available through the denominational offices. Meetings of the deacon fellowship are devoted to reports on family visits and prayer for family needs rather than on the business affairs of the church. The pastor fulfills the equipping role of his ministry and encourages the deacons in fulfilling their pastoral care opportunities.

In a large city church, the pastor had been working for several years to change the nature of deacon service from business to ministry. The size of the church made it impossible for him to relate personally to all of the people, and he believed the deacon family ministry plan would provide the personal touch that the church needed.

Upon hearing of the death of one of his church members, the pastor went immediately to comfort the widow. She welcomed him into the living room where he sought to share her grief. Sitting where she could look out the front window of her home, the widow suddenly sat upright, smiled and exclaimed, "Oh, here comes my minister!" No, she was not out of her mind—the man coming up the walk was her deacon who truly had been her minister during the prolonged illness of her husband. Her preacher was in the living room, but her minister was coming up the walk!

How would you feel at that time? Would you want to say, "Now wait a minute, I'm your minister!" Or would you share the feeling of the pastor involved—"Thank you, Lord, it is working!" His efforts to implement a lay caregiving plan through the deacons was working wonderfully, and he was glad.

The authors of *Lay Caregiving* offer the following principles as fundamental to their own experience with training laypersons for ministry: (1) three elements are essential in training lay caregivers: personal growth, improving caring skills, and integrating theological beliefs and concepts into the practice of caregiving; (2) learners are responsible for their own educational goal setting; (3) learning involves personal experience that is reflected upon, evaluated, and then integrated into the life of the learner; and (4) a learner needs a caring community of other learning caregivers.[5] Churches can draw upon persons in clinical training programs at local hospitals, therapists in private practice, and ministers with pastoral care skills to help guide the training experiences for laypersons.

2. *Families ministering to families.* Apart from the official structures of the church, pastoral care may be given by families to families. Carl and Martha Nelson summarize their chapter on families ministering to families with the observation that creative caring takes "two of you and sometimes your children, your time, your resources, your experiences, your interests and expertise, and at times nothing more than your hearts that have been tendered by the love of Christ—and applies them to the need at hand."[6]

Even though this is an unofficial fulfillment of ministry, families can still be trained through the church's training program to recognize their opportunities for pastoral care and can be given guidance for fulfilling it. The homemaker whose neighbor sits at the kitchen table to unfold a story of hurt and disappointment can give pastoral care at the level of friendship but may need guidance herself in giving suggestions about future possibilities. This can be a vital ministry for the congregation.

---
**Suggested Readings**

Brister, C. W. *Take Care: Translating Christ's Love into a Caring Ministry.* Nashville: Broadman Press, 1978.

Collins, Gary. *How to Be a People Helper.* Ventura, Calif.: Vision House, 1976.

Detwiler-Zapp, Diane and Dixon, W. C. *Lay Caregiving.* Philadelphia: Fortress, 1982.

Nelson, Carl and Martha. *The Ministering Couple: A Plus for any Church.* Nashville: Broadman Press, 1983.

---

### Crisis Counseling

Lofton Hudson defines a crisis as "a situation which has a built-in RSVP!"[7] It is always a situation demanding an answer. Such was the case in an Iowa church when the parents of a high school girl discovered that their daughter was pregnant and asked me to meet with them to discuss it. Their situation illustrates well the interlocking family patterns that can produce crisis as well as serving as an illustration of crisis counseling.

The family had grown up in a Southern city where the daughter had completed all of her schooling through the eleventh grade. Being an outgoing and active girl, she had achieved acceptance into the inner circle of high school leaders and was ready to thoroughly enjoy her senior year in that same high school. At that time, however, her father accepted a transfer to Iowa without giving consideration to the emotional impact that this might have on his daughter. For her, changing schools meant going from being a big wheel in a small school to being a nonperson in a big school.

She was angry with her father but could not express it to him openly. A boy at school sympathized with her, gave her emotional support, and they became sexually intimate. When pregnancy resulted, the parents had to deal with a totally unexpected problem in their church-going family. During the course of the counseling session, the daughter's anger came out, and she acknowledged that her pregnancy was as much an act of retaliation against her father as it was a response to being "loved."

In crisis counseling, however, the immediate situation must take precedence over underlying reasons, so the priority need was to examine options about her pregnancy. After considering the options of abortion, keeping the baby, or giving it up for adoption, the girl decided to enter a maternity home in Missouri, have the baby, and place it for adoption. Arrangements were made for this decision to be implemented. Then the family was able to focus on the family interaction which had helped produce the circumstances favorable to the daughter's pregnancy. Family counseling with the pastor followed crisis counseling with the guest counselor.

This family crisis reflects what Hudson and others describe as the common elements of every crisis: (1) a disturbing or upsetting event, (2) puzzling or painful alternatives, (3) heightened choice anxiety, (4) threat to selfhood, and (5) resolution or resignation. The event was the pregnancy out of wedlock, the painful alternatives have been mentioned, the anxiety over which alternative to choose was evident in the living room of the home, the daughter and parents all felt threat to their selfhood, and the decision to enter the maternity home was the resolution.

Coping with the crisis required personal contact with a ministering person, the reduction of anxiety by definite plans for handling the crisis after focusing on the issue, taking action to implement the decision, then acceptance of each other in God's grace through which father and daughter could forgive each other and plan for a new relationship in the future.

The response to crisis situations may be by the pastor or it may be a lay caregiving situation. Laypersons are effective in crisis ministry whether done over the telephone, as in some community hot lines, or in person through the pastoral care ministry of the church. The range of possible crises is so vast that the pastor needs all the help that he can get to meet family needs. Training lay caregivers for this function extends his ministry greatly.

---

**Suggested Reading**

Bagby, Daniel G. *Transition and Newness*. Nashville: Broadman Press, 1982.

Cole, W. Douglas. *When Families Hurt*. Nashville: Broadman Press, 1979.

Collins, Gary. *How to Be a People Helper*. Ventura, Calif.: Vision House, 1976.

Hudson, R. Lofton. *Persons in Crisis*. Nashville: Broadman Press, 1969.

Switzer, David K. *The Minister as Crisis Counselor*. Nashville: Abingdon, 1974.

---

We have now surveyed ways in which churches can help persons grow toward maturing adulthood, develop strong marriages, grow healthy families, and use the resources of the congregation to meet family needs. Our next task will be to summarize an approach to beginning family ministry in a local church. Since much has already been said about specific activities, chapter 8 will focus on process rather than programs.

# 8
# Organizing
# for Family Ministry

The 1978 survey of Southern Baptist pastors conducted by their Sunday School Board revealed some interesting findings with regard to the pastors' competency in planning family ministry. Of the 192 ministers responding to a question on planning a family ministry program, 11.5 percent indicated they could do this very well, 33.9 percent that they could do it fairly well, and 49.9 percent recognized that they needed training in this area of church leadership. These ministers felt much more comfortable doing crisis ministry and interpreting biblical views of marriage and family relations to their congregations than they did implementing an overall program of family life education and ministry![1]

These findings could probably be replicated among ministers of other denominations as well. It is, therefore, necessary to outline some steps that ministers and/or lay members can take to develop family ministry in a local church. The chart on the next page gives an overview of the process being described.

## Arouse Interest

The first challenge is to arouse interest among the church members and possibly among the church leaders with regard to the needs of families in and out of the church. Sermons that are centered on the contemporary family, as well as illustrations from family life in other sermons, can stimulate interest in what is happening to families in the community as well as the church.

Stories and brief statements on family needs can be included in the weekly or monthly newsletter going to all the members. The effec-

## DEVELOPING A FAMILY LIFE EDUCATION
## AND MINISTRY PROGRAM

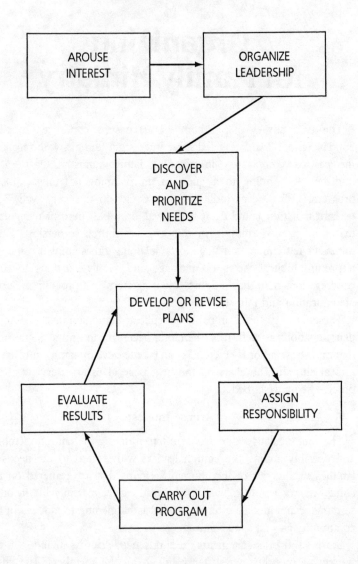

tiveness of these comments can be heightened by including questions concerning the responsibility of the church to help families deal with the issues confronting them in society.

Discuss possibilities for involvement in ministry to families with church groups who have a primary concern for marriage development and parenting responsibilities. Sunday School classes and departments are ideal places to plant seeds of concern in the minds of persons at different stages of the family life cycle. An invitation to conduct a family enrichment conference in Florida came from a pastor whose young adults in Sunday School became concerned for their own family relationships and wanted the church to provide a forum for discussion of family development.

Relate the church's opportunity for ministry to denominational objectives in the family life field. Southern Baptists, for example, have an excellent opportunity to begin programs of family life education and ministry by cooperating with the denomination's 1982-1985 emphasis on strengthening family life through the churches. Their Family Ministry Department is field-testing a parent enrichment program, Parenting by Grace, for use in 1985. The American Baptist Convention department of educational ministries is highlighting sexual education for parents through its Family Sexuality Education Curriculum developed by Joe Leonard and Roger Price. The Nazarene Church through its national headquarters is in a seven-year program developing marriage enrichment leader couples in local churches using an adapted ACME format. The Disciples of Christ (Christian Church) have adopted the Newly-Wed Program first initiated by the Country Club Christian Church, Kansas City, Missouri, as a denominational promotion for couples married up to three years. These examples illustrate the various approaches being made by various denominations to family ministry that can arouse interest.

Interest can be stimulated by personalizing family needs. A Sunday School teacher wanted her class members to participate in ministry to families through a mission chapel sponsored by her church. The women were willing to give money but were not interested in personal ministry to those families. Attitudes changed, however, when the teacher took the class to the mission where they could see the people in person. Then the class members were anxious to do more than give money—they gave themselves to persons in need.

Exposing church members to on-site situations can be done with regard to family ministry needs. Visits to homes for the aging, hospital emergency rooms, law courts where divorce proceedings are being conducted, or homes providing emergency care for children from disturbed families can alert church leaders to community needs for family life education and ministry. Having guest speakers from community agencies that deal with family problems is also effective when on-site visits cannot be accomplished.

### Organize Leadership

When interest is aroused, a typical church member response is, "What can we do about situations like this?" It is then time to organize leadership that can examine ways for the church to respond to that question.

Leadership may come from the regular planning groups of the church such as a Church Council or Church Board. At times persons on that planning group who have a particular interest in family issues will chair an ad hoc committee or task force designed to investigate programs of family ministry in other churches or in their own denomination and report back to the planning group. This investigative committee should be representative of the church constituency so as not to miss any segment of the church in examining possible directions for ministry.

Some churches have found the establishment of a standing committee on family life education and ministry is the best response to the awakened interest of the congregation. Since there probably has been little directed attention to family ministry prior to this time, a standing committee should be empowered to initiate such planning. Members of this committee should be people who have a definite interest in family or the committee will be ineffective. This is definitely not the committee for people who just need a job in church! If church members have particular skills in counseling, teaching in public schools, social work, or other people-oriented specialties, they can be very useful on the family life committee. However, concerned laypeople without such qualifications but who have a desire to learn make effective committee members.

Larger churches have added a person to their staff with a specific assignment in family ministry or have given this assignment to a staff member who will serve as supervisor of the church's program developed by lay committee members. In some situations, a layperson serving in a volunteer capacity is willing to accept this responsibility and actually functions as a staff member when planning is being done on the church calendar.

Any use of lay members requires planned training to equip them for their new responsibilities. Ministers may draw upon the resources of their denominational offices for assistance or may invite family life specialists to assist in the training programs. Preparation of bibliographies for personal study by committee members is also an excellent beginning in this training work.

### Discover and Prioritize Needs

Need discovery is essential to effective family ministry since families may desire forms of ministry not envisioned by the vocational leadership of the church. In the 1978 family needs survey by Southern Baptists, ranking of needs by pastors was often quite different from rankings given by husbands and wives in the congregation. For example, pastors ranked family worship as eleventh whereas couples ranked it first in felt needs. Pastors ranked husband-wife roles in fifth place but couples ranked this issue twelfth and thirteenth in their lists.

In the 1976 Roman Catholic Call to Action Consultation, clergy believed that families wanted more in the way of religious instruction for their children and more direction in fighting abortion. Instead, 825,000 respondents asked for attention to family needs which the clergy hardly dreamed of in planning the activity. The top eight issues compare very closely to the issues reflected in the SBC survey: support of family values, family life education that was more than religious education for children, ministry to divorced persons through the church, teaching communication skills for families, helping families deal with social pressures contrary to good family life, personal and family counseling, developing a family sense of vocation and social witness, and help for single parents.

The committee formed to consider how the Church might respond to these expressed needs kept uppermost in their planning "the constant necessity of listening to families within the parish to determine their real needs before developing parish plans of family ministry."[2]

Discovery of needs can be done through a questionnaire distributed to youth and adults in the church. The following form was distributed to all adults in Sunday School, and the tabulated results were sent to the conference leader. It can be done by having brainstorming sessions with various age groups which gives them opportunity to mention any type of family need that comes to mind. These are usually placed on a chalkboard during the session, consolidated into broad categories of needs, and then tabulated for consideration by the planning committee.

Needs may also be surfaced by committee members reading books on family ministry, as well as books relating to marriage and family development. The latter is especially helpful when tabulating developmental needs that are part of the normal family life cycle. Conversations with families in the church will also highlight felt needs in the congregation. Use some or all of these means to stimulate awareness of needs.

The next step is for the committee to prioritize needs. No church can do all things for everybody and certainly not all at once! Priority may be established on the basis of urgency of need, financial, personnel, and equipment resources available and the willingness of the church to undertake a program of response to the needs surfaced by the committee. The items of highest priority can then be brought to the larger planning group or to the church for consideration before definite plans for implementation are made.

## Develop (or Revise) Plans

The next step depends upon the church's response to the committee's recommendations for action. If the priority listing is accepted as valid, the church calendaring process for establishing immediate, short-range,

The Family Life Conference is an effort to make good marriages better and to improve the quality of life within all families. Would you indicate those items which you feel should have special emphasis during the Family Life Conference. Please place a check on the line before each item which you feel should be discussed during or after the conference.

A. Communication Within Marriage
   ___ Who is boss     ___ Solving differences
B. Areas of Possible Tension
   ___ Role of the husband     ___ Role of the wife
   ___ Working mothers     ___ Finances
C. Parent-Child Relationships
   ___ Discipline of children     ___ Living with the adolescent
   ___ Adolescents living with parents
D. Extended Family Problems
   ___ In-law difficulty
   ___ Belief that one's own heritage and practices are best
E. Sexual
   ___ The Christian perspective on family planning and contraceptives
   ___ Sexual adjustment     ___ Sexuality
   ___ Pre-marital and extra-marital sexuality
F. Sickness and Aging in the Family
   ___ Dealing with emergency and long-term illness
   ___ Planning for death     ___ Preparation for aging
   ___ Caring for parents who are infirm
G. Personal Problems Affecting Family Relationships
   ___ Handling anger
   ___ Problems of personal goals versus family goals
   ___ Self-realization within the family
H. Problem Areas Related to the Adult Life Cycle
   ___ Preparation for marriage
   ___ Early years of marriage     ___ Middle years of marriage
   ___ Later years of marriage and retirement
I. Other Areas—Be Specific
   _____

   _____

Please review all the above broad areas (A-I) and rank each area with either of the scores below:
1—most important     2—second in importance     3—least important
Check Age Group 20-24___, 25-34___, 45-54___, 55-74___.

and long-term goals of ministry will need to begin. A crucial aspect of planning is the church's financial commitment to the program which then gives the family life committee specific authority to develop plans.

For example, the family life committee recommends that an activity of first priority is to conduct a family enrichment conference designed to offer help for people in all stages of the family life cycle. They are ready to proceed with plans for such a conference but will need to know what financial resources are available to enlist leadership for the group and general sessions. Upon receiving assurance of available money, the committee can then work with the church council to project a date in the church calendar that is far enough in the future to allow adequate planning time for the activity. When a date is confirmed, actual definition of tasks can be made.

### Carry Out the Program

Planning leads to action. The committee members or task force leaders will oversee the actual implementation of the program through the threefold schedule of preparation, promotion, and performance. Naturally the type of activity planned will influence what these three terms involve.

### Evaluate Results

Churches do not complete the process of planning if they neglect evaluation of the activity. The schedule of upcoming activities captures their attention with the result that appropriate evaluative measures are not used for the purpose of revising, strengthening, or scrapping programs that have been completed.

Evaluation can be immediate or delayed, it can be by participants or by observers, it can be oral or written, but it needs to be done. Immediate evaluation by questionnaire is a valuable resource for future planning. Conference leaders know that time must be provided in the schedule for these evaluative questionnaires to be completed and turned in before people leave the session or the response may be minimal. The questionnaire on the next page illustrates how people may be invited to judge an activity.

FOLLOW-UP QUESTIONNAIRE
FAMILY CONFERENCE

Now that you have experienced the Family Conference, we would appreciate some feedback that may help us when we plan future conferences. Please check the workshop group you attended:

\_\_ (a)  The Two of Us
\_\_ (b)  Single Parenting
\_\_ (c)  Family of One
\_\_ (d)  Living Creatively with Children
\_\_ (e)  Living Creatively with Teens
\_\_ (f)  Free at Last—The Kids are Gone
\_\_ (g)  Middle-Aged Children of Aged Parents
\_\_ (h)  Growing in Retirement
\_\_ (i)  None of the Above
\_\_ (j)  Youth Session
\_\_ (k)  Children's Session

1. How did you hear about this conference?

2. What is the most interesting, helpful aspect of the conference.

3. What would you change? Do you have new or different ideas about things that might be included in a family conference to make it even more effective?

4. If follow-up groups such as these interest groups are formed, would you be interested \_\_ somewhat interested \_\_ very interested \_\_ in being included?
   Name_____
   Address_____
   Phone Number_____

Oral evaluation by program leaders as well as selected participants is an effective reflective tool. Letting the leaders know that such evaluation will be requested encourages them to be more observant of process during the program.

Delayed evaluation after participants have had time to think about their experience is also an excellent input for program revision. Here again informing them of this desire will aid recall and constructive criticism.

After committee reflection on the various evaluative inputs, a report can be made to the larger planning committee or to the church with recommendations for continuance, revision, or cessation of the activity under consideration.

Thus the planning cycle moved from discovered needs to plans to assignment of responsibility to carrying out the program to evaluation and then back to revision or adoption of new plans. Each stage of the cycle is essential to success in organizing for family ministry.

───────────Suggested Reading───────────

Feucht, Oscar E., ed. *Helping Families Through the Church.* Saint Louis: Concordia, 1957.

Hinkle, Joseph W. and Cook, Melva J. *How to Minister to Families in Your Church.* Nashville: Broadman Press, 1978.

Leonard, Joe. *Planning Family Ministry In a Teaching Church.* Valley Forge, PA.: Judson Press, 1982.

Louthan, Sheldon and Martin, Grant. *Family Ministries in Your Church.* Glendale, Calif.: G/L Publications, 1977.

Sell, Charles M. *Family Ministry: The Enrichment of Family Life Through the Church.* Grand Rapids: Zondervan, 1981.

Smith, Leon. *Family Ministry: An Educational Resource for the Local Church.* Nashville: Discipleship Resources, 1975.

Sunday School Board of the Southern Baptist Convention. *The Church Family Ministry Committee.* Nashville: BSSB, 1981.

Wynn, John Charles. *Pastoral Ministry to Families.* Philadelphia: Westminster, 1967.

# Notes

CHAPTER 1

1. (Nashville: The Sunday School Board of the Southern Baptist Convention, 1980), p. 2.

2. See Joseph W. Hinkle, Ron Johnson and Charles M. Lowry, *Oikos: A Practical Approach to Family Evangelism* (Nashville: Broadman Press, 1982) for suggestions on implementing this objective.

3. C. W. Brister, *Take Care: Translating Christ's Love into a Caring Ministry.* (Nashville: Broadman Press, 1978), p. 13.

4. Joseph W. Hinkle and Melva J. Cook, *How to Minister to Families in Your Church* (Nashville: Broadman Press, 1978), pp. 115-116.

5. See Carl and Martha Nelson, *The Ministering Couple: A Plus for Any Church* (Nashville: Broadman Press, 1983) for a helpful discussion of families ministering to families.

CHAPTER 2

1. Bill Moulder, "Living Alone," *Voices* (Fall 1978), p. 4.

2. Evelyn Duvall, *Family Development*, 3rd Ed. (Philadelphia: J. B. Lippincott Co., 1967), p. vi.

CHAPTER 3

1. J. C. Wynn, *Pastoral Ministry to Families* (Philadelphia: Westminster Press, 1967), p. 26.

2. Russell Dicks, *Pastoral Work and Personal Counseling* (New York: The Macmillan Co., 1947), p. 202.

3. John Killinger, *The Centrality of Preaching in the Total Task of Ministry* (Waco: Word Books, 1969), pp. 28, 60.

4. Harry Emerson Fosdick, "What's the Matter with Preaching?" *Harpers* (July 1929), mimeographed copy.

5. Edgar N. Jackson, *How to Preach to People's Needs* (Nashville: Abingdon Press, 1956), p. 14.

6. *Family Ministry Needs in Local Churches* (Nashville: The Sunday School Board of the Southern Baptist Convention, 1978), p. 8.

7. Killinger, p. 63.

8. Kenneth Chafin, *Is There a Family in the House?* (Waco: Word Books, 1978), p. 31.

9. John R. Claypool, *Stages* (Waco: Word Books, 1977), p. 15.

10. David Mace, "Marriage in Transition: Implications for Social Policy," *Pastoral Psychology* (Summer 1977), p. 241.

CHAPTER 4

1. John A. Ishee, *From Here to Maturity* (Nashville: Broadman Press, 1974), p. 15.

2. Robert Schuller, *Self-Esteem: The New Reformation* (Waco: Word Books, 1982), p. 35.

3. Ibid., pp. 17-18.

4. *Holiday Inn Companion* (April-May 1975), p. 8.

5. Roy Lee Honeycutt, Jr., *Crisis and Response* (New York: Abingdon Press, 1965), p. 21.

6. Schuller, p. 100.

7. Sidney Jourard, *The Transparent Self* (New York: Van Nostrand Reinhold, 1971), p. 11.

8. W. Wayne Grant, *Growing Parents Growing Children* (Nashville: Convention Press, 1977), pp. 55-56.

9. Don Dinkmeyer and Gary D. McKay, STEP Publishers' Building, Circle Pines, Minnesota 55014.

10. Erik H. Erikson, "Eight Stages of Man," *Childhood and Society* (Middlesex: England: Penguin Books, 1965), pp. 252-253.

11. Craig W. Ellison, ed., *Your Better Self: Christianity, Psychology and Self-Esteem* (A Harper/CAPS Book; San Francisco: Harper and Row, 1983), p. 12.

12. "Eleven Million Singles: Their Joys and Frustrations," *U.S. News and World Report* (Feb. 21, 1983). Information in the chart is from the US Department of Commerce.

13. Arland Thorton and Deborah Freedman, *Marriage and Divorce Today* (January 3, 1983), p. 3.

14. Donna L. Peterson, "Life Is for Singles Too," *Voices* (Winter 1981), pp. 5-6.

CHAPTER 5

1. Jimmy Smith, *The Baptist Program* (June-July, 1978), p. 6.

2. Claude A. Guldner, "Marriage Preparation and Marriage Enrichment: The Preventive Approach," *Pastoral Psychology* (Summer 1977), pp. 248-259.

3. E. Clifton Davis, Alan J. Hovestadt, Fred P. Piercy, and Samuel W. Cochran, "Effects of Weekend and Weekly Marriage Enrichment Program Formats," *Family Relations* (January 1982), pp. 85-89.

4. See "Getting Serious About Marriage Improvement," *Leadership 100* (July-August, 1983), pp. 8-10.

5. Wayne E. Oates, ed., *An Introduction to Pastoral Counseling* (Nashville: Broadman Press, 1959), p. vi.

6. Samuel Shoemaker, *How You Can Help Other People* (New York: E. P. Dutton & Co., 1946), p. 23.

7. J. C. Wynn, *Family Therapy in Pastoral Ministry* (San Francisco: Harper and Row, 1982), p. 111.

Chapter 6

1. J. C. Wynn, *Family Therapy in Pastoral Ministry* (San Francisco: Harper and Row, 1982), chapter 2.

2. Michael H. Elmore, "Family Life Emphasis: a Case Report," *Church Administration* (April 1973), pp. 23-25.

3. Milton L. Rudnick, *Christian Ethics for Today: An Evangelical Approach* (Grand Rapids: Baker, 1979), pp. 28, 29.

4. *Ten Reasons Why Adopted Children Tend to Have More Conflicts* (Institute in Basic Youth Conflicts: 1982), pp. 1, 2.

5. The Baptist Faith and Message, Article III, Man.

6. E. Y. Mullins, *The Christian Religion in its Doctrinal Expression* (Philadelphia: Judson, 1917), pp. 285-302.

7. Alan Richardson, ed., *A Theological Wordbook of the Bible* (New York: The Macmillan Co., 1950), p. 14.

8. Roger Bishop, Davene Cohen, Samellyn Wood, *Parenting: Four Patterns of Child-Rearing* (New York: A & W Visual Library, 1978).

9. Frances L. Ilg, Louise Bates Ames, and Sidney M. Baker, *Child Behavior*, rev. ed. (New York: Harper and Row, 1981).

10. Virginia Satir, *Peoplemaking* (Palo Alto, Calif.: Science and Behavior Books. 1972).

11. Thomas Gordon, *Parent Effectiveness Training* (New York: Peter H. Wyden, 1970).

12. Dale Keeton, *Strengthening Families* (Nashville: Christian Life Commission of The Southern Baptist Convention, 1982), p. 4.

13. Oscar E. Feuchts, "The Word in Your House," *Worship in the Family* (St. Louis: Concordia, n.d.), p. 1.

14. Ernst and Clara Klein, *Bible Reading and Worship in the Home* (Valley Forge, Pa.: Department of Adult Work and Family Life, 1963).

15. David Edens, *Marriage: How to Have It the Way You Want It* (Englewood Cliffs, N.J.: Prentice-Hall, 1982), p. 32.

16. William Kaufman, "Some Emotional Uses of Money," *Pastoral Psychology* (April 1965), pp. 43-53.

17. Susan Bondy, "Bondy: Mind Over Money," *Money* (October 1982), pp. 66-67.

Chapter 7

1. Douglas A. Anderson, *New Approaches to Family Pastoral Care* (Philadelphia: Fortress Press, 1980), p. 69.

2. J. C. Wynn, *Family Therapy in Pastoral Ministry* (San Francisco: Harper and Row, 1982), p. 93.

3. Samuel L. Shoemaker, *How You Can Help Other People* (New York: E.P. Dutton & Co., 1946), p. 18.

4. Henry Webb, *Deacons: Servant Model in the Church* (Nashville: Convention Press, 1980), pp. 8, 76.

5. Diane Detwiler-Zapp and W. C. Dixon, *Lay Caregiving* (Philadelphia: Fortress, 1982), pp. 48-49.

6. Carl and Martha Nelson, *The Ministering Couple: A Plus for Any Church* (Nashville: Broadman Press, 1983), p. 46.

7. R. Lofton Hudson, *Persons in Crisis* (Nashville: Broadman Press, 1969), p. 5.

CHAPTER 8

1. BSSB, *Family Ministry Needs,* p. 8.

2. Delores Curran, "Family Ministry and the Parish: Barriers and Visions," *Family Ministry,* eds. Gloria Duke and Joanmarie Smith (Oak Grove, Minn.: Winston Press, 1980), pp. 8-11.